Leadership for Social Justice, Volume VI

A PLACE to Call Home

Authored by students in
JPST 365 Leadership for Social Justice, Fall 2019
Justice and Peace Studies Program
University of St. Thomas

Edited by Dr. Mike Klein

Cover art and interior art by Sarah Nelson
Cover design by Dr. Mike Klein

Order at: amazon.com

Table of Contents

Acknowledgements

The authors would like to express our thanks to:
Sustainable Communities Partnership at the University of St. Thomas, for developing a multi-year partnership with PLACE.
Joshua Crespo and Ashmita Geyerman who contributed to our collective work in our course and in support of this book.
Sarah Nelson, Artist in Residence in the Sustainable Communities Partnership, for teaching us to speak without words, and for her phenomenal and captivating art, and for her collaborative and empathetic work with us in the classroom to capture ideas through shared visual imagery.
Jamie Marshall and St. Louis Park Friends of the Arts
Sabathani Community Center
Jim McDonough for wisdom and perspective
Jeanne Seely Smith for giving college students your time
Edgar Rudberg for your honesty and knowledge
Gretchen Nicholls
Kevin Ehrman Solberg
Professor Paul Lorah
Maria Wardoku
Carley Rice
John Bardi
Our professor, Mike Klein
…and the people of PLACE, for your openness to this collaboration, your integrity in the process, and your vision of housing that promotes social and environmental justice, including Chris Velsasco, Abby Alldaffer, Todd Bagby, Alice Hiniker, and Elizabeth Bowling.

About the Artist – Sarah Nelson

The phenomenal art that graces the cover and appears throughout the book was created by Sarah Nelson, an artist in residence supported by the Sustainable Communities Partnership in the Office of Sustainability Initiatives at the University of St. Thomas. Sarah is a visual artist formerly based in St. Paul and currently operates from Los Angeles, California.

In her work, Sarah invites the viewer to come in closer, using intricate detail to create intimacy between her colors, line work, and her audience.

Her work is increasingly focused around environmental concerns. She operates a monthly illustrated and researched digital environmental resource, called 'This Amazing Planet'. She also creates fine art based on environmental topics for various exhibitions around the country.

Commissions and collaborations have included illustrations for the Public Works Minneapolis, North Country Cottages, Cavalier Coastal Kitchen, Corner Table, the City Pages, Dead Man Winter, Odd Bird, Five Watt Coffee, and has works in private collections around the world.

Find out more about Sarah Nelson's art at:
https://sarahnelson.art/
https://www.worksbysarahnelson.com/

Introduction

The stories collected in this volume are generated from the work of undergraduate students in a course entitled Leadership for Social Justice (JPST 365). This writing-intensive course in the Justice and Peace Studies Program at the University of St. Thomas (Minnesota, USA) creates an opportunity for students to compose a book chapter over the course of a semester framed by three assignments (see Pedagogy below). Each of the chapters follows a common format: story, theory, collective action, works cited and an author's biography.

We entered into this collaboration with PLACE because of its example of leadership for social justice in housing. As described on their website https://www.welcometoplace.org, "PLACE is a 501(c)(3) nonprofit team collaborating with cities to design and build mixed-income, transit-oriented developments that feature the arts and affordable living opportunities." PLACE had partnered with other University of St. Thomas classes previously through our Sustainable Communities Partnership. By grounding our education in this practical example of leadership, students and I could move beyond abstract concepts and generalizations to learn through a praxis orientation, the interplay of theory and practice. PLACE operates with this same orientation toward education and action that informs their planning, community engagement, and development work.

The approach to leadership in this course - and in this book – requires some description and definition of key terms. **Leadership** is not based on positional or individual leadership, as is so often the presumption of leadership theory that focuses on traits or characteristics. Instead leadership is described through the dynamics of power, operating between individuals in community, with different identities, and enacting collective agency to affect change. These stories do not ignore the role of individual leaders exercising power. Instead, the individual is de-centered to focus on how power operates in the relationships between individuals, groups, and systems. Leadership is a verb more than it is a noun.

Social justice is the ability for people to participate in the decisions that most impact their lives. It is defined by recognition of rights and responsibilities in an organization, community, or society, and by distribution of income and wealth such that everyone has the opportunity to live and thrive.

Peacebuilding is the structural work to create the conditions for social justice. In the field of peace studies, peace is defined as the absence of violent conflict (negative peace), and as the presence of just relationships and systems to deal with conflict nonviolently and promote human flourishing (positive peace). Peacebuilding is proactive work to develop the structures that support positive peace, prevent violent conflict, and increase human agency.

And this book requires some normative framing. Students chose the title of this book to describe their collected work. They present individual stories of people connected to housing in order to narrate a larger collective story about the role of housing in sustainability and social justice. Students write to re-present voices authentically, and describe peacebuilding responsibly, hoping they will encourage and inspire you, reader, to enact your own leadership for social justice.

The tree motif on the book cover was developed from the visual imagery the authors found in their stories, and synthesized in collaboration with artist, Sarah Nelson. In *A PLACE to Call Home*, the tree represents: transformation and growth through systems change, diversity in the common need for housing in particular communities, acknowledgment of ancestral and contemporary Dakota land, the scar of redlining in racial and ethnic and religious minority communities, and our own growth in understanding housing's role in social justice.

We realized through this work that housing is central to historical movements for social justice and we came to know the current urgent issues – the Stories of Now – connected to housing: stories of equity and dignity, stories of policy and practice, stories of relationship and community. We expect that you will find these themes woven throughout this volume, and that your own stories will rise in response to those you read here.

As their professor and editor, I hope this volume provides an opportunity for you to know the voice of students as they enact their own learning and as they advance their own leadership through storytelling. I am proud of their work and hopeful for the transformations of individuals and communities through leadership for social justice in the pursuit of peace.

Mike Klein

Pedagogy

The profiles collected here provide diverse and remarkable accounts of housing and social justice. They also represent the work of students as they learn about leadership in the context of this pressing social issue. Several pedagogical elements of this course are foundational to the stories presented below and are described here to add context to the process underlying this text.

Writing in the Disciplines

Under an institutional Writing Across the Curriculum (WAC) program, Writing in the Disciplines projects are founded on specialized skills student develop in order to write effectively in different academic disciplines and associated professions. Each assignment encourages students to practice writing in formats that reflect the discipline and prepare them for professional writing. It is product-driven approach to learning that sets a high bar for student achievement. In particular, this assignment calls on students to be ethical and authentic in their representation of the voices of their profile subject. They must also be responsible for a profile that is published and publicly available, and accountable to the subject of their profile. Students must achieve a minimum standard of quality, reflected through their course grade, to be included in this publication. A classroom protocol for student research was approved by the University of St. Thomas Institutional Review Board (IRB# 819449-5).

The Circle of Praxis

This pedagogical model is based on the work of Brazilian educator Paulo Freire. As a literacy educator in Brazil, Freire developed a praxis approach to education that went beyond knowledge to empower students for liberation from oppressive systems. This methodology is presented in Freire's *Pedagogy of the Oppressed* (1970) and subsequent works (1973, 1985, 1998), and further developed in liberation theology (Guttierez, 1988; Ellacuria & Sobrino, 1993). A particular form of praxis pedagogy, the Circle of Praxis (Smith & Haasl, 1999), is central to my own research and teaching (Klein, 2013, 2016; Klein, Finnegan & Nelson-Pallmeyer, 2018). The Circle of Praxis is a concise yet expansive approach to education that informs the course that generated this text, and it structures this collection of stories in four parts:

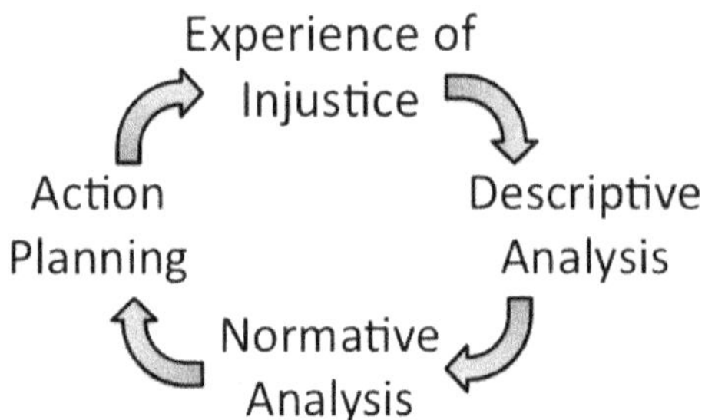

The Circle of Praxis is made up of four broad educational steps. This methodology begins in the *experience of injustice,* starting from the margins of power, and in solidarity with people subject to oppression. Experience may be direct or vicarious through first-hand accounts, primary sources, or other media, like this text. In the second step, experience is subjected to *descriptive analysis*

through the social sciences, especially history, sociology, economics and political science. In the third step, descriptions are interpreted through *normative analysis* to examine worldviews, religious perspectives, assumptions, and constructions of meaning that describe power differentials and promote ethical collective agency to make change. The fourth step, *action planning,* develops strategies that promote justice and peace, and tactics that account for available resources, potential obstacles, allies and adversaries. And this last step leads to the next experience in the cycle.

Courses in the Department of Justice and Peace Studies are framed by Circle of Praxis pedagogy. Leadership for Social Justice is grounded in the stories of people facing injustice and oppression in order to see empathetically (if imperfectly) from that perspective. Then descriptive and normative analyses provide understanding for action planning. Our goal is not just to know the world, but also to act in the world to advance common goods.

This is the primary pedagogical model for the course Leadership for Social Justice, and the primary framework for this book. Transit transformation stories are grouped into experiences of transit, descriptive analysis, normative analysis, and action planning: all to give texture and meaning to the role of transit in sustainable communities.

Works Cited

Ellacuria, I. & Sobrino, J. (1993). Mysterium liberationis: Fundamental   concepts of liberation theology. Maryknoll, NY: Orbis

Freire, P. (1970/1990). Pedagogy of the oppressed. New York: Continuum.

______. (1973). Education for critical consciousness. New York: Continuum.

______. (1985). The politics of education: Culture, power, and liberation. New York: Bergin & Garvey.

______. (1998). Pedagogy of freedom: Ethics, democracy, and civic courage. Lanham, MD: Rowman & Littlefield.

Gutierrez, G., (1988). A theology of liberation: History, politics, and salvation. Maryknoll, N.Y: Orbis Books.

Klein, Mike. (2013). "Cell phones, T-shirts and Coffee: Codification of Commodities in a Circle of Praxis Pedagogy." *Peace Studies Journal Special Edition: The Business of War and Peace, and the Potential for Education to Play a Transformative Role*, 6(1) 31-45.

Klein, Mike. (2016). *Democratizing Leadership: Counter-Hegemonic Democracy in Communities, Organizations, and Institutions*. Vol. 1 of Counter-Hegemonic Democracy and Social Change. Charlotte, NC: Information Age Publishing.

Klein, M.; Finnegan, A; Nelson-Pallmeyer, J. (2017). "Circle of Praxis Pedagogy for Peace Studies." *Peace Review, Issue 30(3): Designing Peace and War Curricula.*

Smith, David. W. & Haasl, Mike. (1999). "Justice and Peace Studies at the University of St. Thomas", In Weigart, Kathleen M., Crews, Robin J. *Teaching for justice: Concepts and Models for Service-learning in Peace Studies*. Washington, D.C: American Association for Higher Education

History

"booshke giin" but I am not sure.

This means, it's up to you or its your choice in Ojibwe

What do we do with the Truth? Do you know the history of the land you are standing, sitting, or laying on as you read this? If not, you should really go find out before you continue reading. No, seriously if you have not and want to read on, please do it (see Appendix A). Now that you know, lets continue. Do you know where your grandmothers were born and what ancestral lands you belong to? Do you know how you have gained the things (purposefully or not) you have in this country and what roles your ancestors played in passing them down to you? I urge you to deeply ponder this question with full honesty as it is crucial to understanding where you fit into this story. This story is about colonization, decolonization, indigenization, our country, your homelands (wherever that may be for you), the world, and truth. If you are confused as to why you're reading a piece about decolonization in a book about housing, the act of decolonization is in place! If you struggle with this piece of writing, I encourage you to do so and understand the root of the struggle.

If you do not know the history of our nation in regards of indigenous peoples, once again, please educate yourself first (see

Appendix B). Not many educational institutions allow honest history to be taught, so I do not blame you if you are confused. Please read resources that allow Native American voices to lift up the truth of the United States, their truth of the United States. Once you are informed and have an understanding of the United States history of oppression, genocide, and forced assimilation upon Native Americans, we can move onto the next step. The next step is understanding where you fit into that system of colonization. Where were your ancestors in this process and what have you gained or lost because of the establishment of the United States of America? This can be very tricky for many that are non-indigenous in understanding how generational privileges are passed down and manifest from generation to generation. Whether you are of settler, indigenous, newly immigrated lineage (in that case, welcome), or any other mix that fits into colonization, you need to find where you fit into the story. There is trauma on all sides of this process, we are all colonized peoples and cannot escape the foundations with which we all live in now. If you identify with settler origins it is important to know that it is not your fault, however it is your responsibility to help with this process of decolonization. If you are uncomfortable with this truth, you should be, it is in no way what the Manifest Destiny told you to believe. Your entire ontology is being dismantled and that can be disturbing.

By way of lineage and being in the United States, you are directly connected to colonization. So now that you know this, why should you care? My biggest answer to this is because the systems of colonization (that most of the world operates under) and capitalism will only fuel the ecological catastrophe that we all will experience in one way or another. So, what the hell are we supposed to do? How do we fix this deep-rooted system that we all are forced to participate in? I ask myself this question every day and I'm going to tell you there is no one singular one and done solution to decolonization. Just because it is not simple does not mean that there are no tangible and easy tasks to take on. One of the biggest efforts to decolonize is taking down the axiology that came along with settlers and colonizers. Axiology is the study of what is valued, which shapes our ethics and what we choose to give time to. That axiology is in place today and can be challenging to really see and dismantle. For example, newness is prized in American society. The newest iPhone, gaming console, or celebrity is always highly valued. I am not asserting that new things are not valuable, they are. This process of creating lifesaving and/or revolutionary ideas/things is great! But what do we do with the old things that are no longer new? Why can't we create things so that we will not have to make a new thing to replace in x amount of time? What is the reason that we need to shift so quickly from one popular idea to the next, why do we place value on new things even if they aren't good at all?

The reason I mention this particularly valued characteristic of newness is the movement to create land acknowledgements. Land acknowledgments are fairly new and seem to be quite popular. When they are done in a way that does not seek to move to a place of innocence, they can be powerful and create a snowball of change. Because land acknowledgements are so new and could seem to be a fad, I deeply fear that these acknowledgements will only be done to support the status quo valuation because it is new. Land acknowledgements seek to tell the truth of the land and which tribe has had that specific land stolen and appropriated. Land acknowledgements are simply a proclamation of truth that is inescapably tied to the land. The truth of the land is new to many people, but I assure you, it is not new to indigenous peoples. So, once again, what are we supposed to do with this truth, now that it is being told in a way that is equitable to all? How do we talk about these truths without victimizing the native peoples of that land? Who gets a say in what this process looks like? These land acknowledgments are the first step to decolonization. There is no point to telling the truth of our country if we do not honor it. Only telling the truth is like the doctor telling you, you have an illness and providing no treatment. There must be efforts made by people that are not indigenous to honor the truth of their country. Truth only has one voice, we cannot make a new one after indigenous truth is widely circulated in the public.

Where PLACE fits into this is how they will decide to do their land acknowledgement for their building and what steps they will take to further decolonize their space and actions. PLACE seems to have great intentions, but sometimes that is not enough to ensure that there is positive impact. During my interview with Chris Valesco, the executive director, and Abby Alldaffer, another member of the team, we wrestled with how to make the intentions of their land acknowledgement match the impact they hope to have. Once again, there really is no finite solution to this moral dilemma, but there is critical thinking that can be done to honor the truth. A story about this process comes to mind when addressing these good intentions that surfaces when ontological ethics arise. This story is a precautionary tale about those that want to do good and have good intentions but fail in the end because they do not understand their true implications.

In a speech given by Monsignor Ivan Illich to the Conference on InterAmerican Student Projects he addresses voluntary sacrifices that are given with intentions of making others' lives better. This speech was given in 1968 in Cuernavaca, Mexico in efforts to address the imposing of American justice and our way of life. Illich begins with an explanation of his speech, "I did not come here to argue. I am here to tell you, if possible, to convince you, and hopefully, to stop you, from pretentiously imposing yourselves on Mexicans" (Illich, 1968). There is a paradox that must be addressed within the room. The intentions of making a poor Mexicans life better, is ridiculous when those efforts are seen through volunteer mission trips and not fully understanding the needs of the people. The good intentions of these people may not always seem so great, when the outcomes do not align with the intent. There are land acknowledgements to be made and intentions to be questioned. In Illich's speech I am reminded of the American tendency to be ethnocentric in ways that are unknown to them. Because America treasures ideas and objects that are new, there seems to be a push to create land acknowledgements with the intention of being politically correct. This push is greatly questioned by me for many reasons. I wonder if there has been a strong input on what indigenous people think is fair when land acknowledgements are created. There are many different ways to say sorry and be sorry, but what about "doing sorry?" Yes, we can walk around and tell the truth about our countries until every ear receives the message, but what happens after that? We are not quite at that point yet, nor are we at the point of accepting what the truth actually is. If the intentions of telling the truth and acknowledging what was done is genuine and seeks reconciliation, then there will be a much longer conversation. The process of this conversation must be respected for we cannot just heal from trauma in short periods of time. Though we can never fully decolonize, there are great ways in which we can ask the parties that were the main subjects of colonization about their needs in accepting the apology. The narrative must remain that indigenous peoples are in charge of this process. How we create that is based around when we understand that good intentions do not mean justice. If we do not understand that intentions should be questioned and do not excuse accidental harms, then these intentions could add to the issues that originally sought to mend. I fear that a false or well-intended land acknowledgement may push away indigenous peoples and their own ideas of reconciliation. Uplifting indigenous voices and their relationship in this "doing of sorry" must be honored, for it helps well assuming non-indigenous folks understand that this sorry is really not about them. This is the first step to doing sorry and what comes next must be in direct junction to indigenous people's true ideas of restorative and meaningful justice.

Works Cited:

Illich, I. (1968, April). To Hell With Good Intentions. Conference on
InterAmerican Student Projects. Cuernavaca. Retrieved from
http://www.swaraj.org/illich_hell.htm

Appendix: A

Visit: https://native-land.ca/

Appendix B

Before Columbus (Native American Documentary) Timeline
Decolonization Is for Everyone | Nikki Sanchez | TEDxSFU
Pedagogy of the Decolonizing | Quetzala Carson | TEDxUAlberta

About the Author – Savannah Thibert

Boozhoo. Savannah Thibert nindizhnikaaz. Obahshiing nindoojbaa. My name is Savannah Thibert and I am member of the Turtle Mountain Band of Chippewa and was raised in Ponemah, Minnesota on the Red Lake Reservation. I will pursue tribal law after I finish my undergraduate degree. I hope to protect treaties and re-obtain land after I finish law school.

Given a Chance... (Part I)

We remain committed to the belief that when a mother is empowered by the human spirit, hope within her awakens - and a cycle breaks.
- Perspectives Family, 'Our Story'

She is a drug addict in the middle of an opioid crisis. She has mental health issues. She is depressed. She is homeless. She is a mother. In our nation and in our communities, we fail to recognize the impact of each of these aspects working together against a woman. From her point of view, she is trapped in a cycle that only harms her and her children repetitively, but there seems to be no way to break it. Imagine this woman. It is impossible for us to feel it, but try to picture the fear, the hopelessness, the fog, the desperation she feels when faced with a system that sees her as another statistic of homelessness, one more number added to the impoverished. Imagine her child. Just a baby, or a toddler, a teenager dealing with the beginnings of the same cycle of mental illness, substance abuse, and homelessness. Maybe she has two children, or even three; she is pulled tight with worry and fear because she can barely provide for herself, let alone her children.

Cue Perspectives-Family. Cue PLACE. Cue an entire community of people that want to create just opportunities for women like her, people like this. Perspectives-Family is an organization located in St. Louis Park, Minnesota that is dedicated to supporting women as they rebuild each aspect of their lives. By housing over 75 women and 130 children per year, this therapeutic housing program is instilling a greater sense of social justice and empowerment within families. Focusing on her mental health, her physical health, her education, her quality of life, and the well-being of her children, this human service program creates ripples in the still waters of our passive society. Providing these services to women trapped in the cycle of poverty gives them and their children another chance at a better life.

Women like her are brought in directly from Hennepin County homeless shelters and placed into 1 of 53 fully furnished apartments. These apartments have fully stocked kitchen, beds and bedding for children and mother, furniture, toiletries, and groceries. All of the functional aspects that make up a higher quality of life are provided through Perspectives' campaign Furnishing Hope. This campaign relies heavily upon donors and fundraising as a means to acquire the apartments and their furnishings; but it is of utmost importance in creating a solid foundation for these healing families to grow. As quoted by Perspectives, "creating a safe, comfortable and nurturing environment is the first step for a mother and her children to rebuild what poverty, addiction and mental illness has taken away" (Perspectives Family, 2019)

In an interview with the CEO of Perspectives-Family, Jeannie Seeley Smith, she stressed that Perspectives-Family recognizes the intersectionality between mental health and substance abuse. The two simply cannot be treated or evaluated as effectively alone as they can when seen as one feeding into the other. Seeley Smith stated:

Until 20 years ago, mental health and chemical dependency were at odds with each other, almost bitter enemies. Mental health did not give credence to the simplicity of the 12 Step Program in alcoholics anonymous, and somebody who was in [chemical dependency] recovery did not benefit from counseling. In fact, they only benefitted from somebody who had a life experience like that (personal communication, November 20, 2019).

This is why Perspectives-Family offers both substance use and mental health treatment within their clinical services. Because women in this cycle of poverty would face deep mental health issues and trauma, they often medicated themselves with what was all too available: drugs and alcohol.

This woman is stuck within drug abuse, trauma, and mental illness and no perceivable way to combat them. Perspectives-Family focuses on helping the mother improve her life through mental health assessments, individual and family psychotherapy, group psychotherapy, chemical health outpatient treatment, counseling, and further treatment plans. Through teaching, counseling, and a supportive community, women take back their own agency and power to break out of the cycle and grow from their experience.

You have been picturing this woman in all of her dead ends; but now look to her child. Let's say he is a three-year-old little boy, just beginning to process new information and to understand vaguely what is going on around him. When mom is dealing with homelessness, depression, and an opioid addiction it hits him hard. It is traumatic and it dictates each aspect of his life, which is only just beginning. When asked about her start at Perspectives-Family, Seeley Smith commented:

As soon as we did the supportive housing program, we realized 'what are we going to do with all these kids', because they were stealing cars and smoking pot and running away. They got their moms back and they felt safe again. They no longer had to be the parent to the mom, so they became the child and then they were acting out. So, we said we needed to have a place for them. And that's why we built the Family Center (personal communication, November 20, 2019).

Seeley Smith was excited to speak about the expansion of the Family Center, a 13 million dollar project. The organization is in the process of requesting the final 4.5 million dollars to complete the expansion which would hold incredible developments for the children of at-risk mothers. The expanded family development center will foster a larger Kids Connection, a program focused on kindergarten through 8th grade students that provides education on multiple scales. It is designed to allow kids to be kids in an environment that furthers their social and academic lives. The focus on the child is just as important as the focus on the mother. Family ties are what help women and their children out of the unjust cycle of poverty, homelessness, mental illness, and drug abuse.

Relationships, interdependence, acknowledgement of the unity between human beings. Mother and the child, a woman and her community, human relationships. These must become the fundamental building blocks of community development. According to John Kretzmann and John P. McKnight, and their Asset-Based Community Development model, "The hard truth is that development must start from within the community and, in most of our urban neighborhoods, there is no other choice" (Kretzmann, McKnight; 1996). The whole premise behind asset-based community development is to focus on the good, the relationships, and the resources a community already possesses, as opposed to focusing on what the community or target group lacks and making their deficits the sole illuminated aspect of their development. Therefore, "as a result, many lower income urban neighborhoods are now environments of service where behaviors are affected because residents come to believe that their well-being depends upon being a client. They begin to see themselves as people with special needs that can only be met by outsiders. They become consumers of services, with no incentive to be producers" (Kretzmann, McKnight; 1996). With Perspectives-Family, this method of highlighting the skills already inherent within the target group and the relationships in between becomes a way to break the cycle of poverty among homeless women and children facing mental illness and substance abuse.

Perspectives-Family is centered around supportive, transitional housing for homeless women and their children. There are basic needs that have to be met in terms of food, clothing, shelter, and human compassion. While this closely follows the path of needs-based community development - a method that, when standing alone, can create a dependent community rather than an independent and self-sustaining community - it is still vitally important to address. However, when this needs-based model is fulfilled hand in hand with asset-based community development, a whole dynamic of active change is set into motion. With basic needs met, women in this program are finally able to build on and strengthen relationships between their children and their communities.

Perspectives-Family supportive services such as substance abuse counseling, treatment, and psychological evaluations address the deficits or needs within a marginalized group of people. They then move on to facilitate inter-generational connection and education. The focus on both the mother and the child as both individuals and woven together in relationship relies heavily on asset-based development. Kretzmann and McKnight claim, "If a community development process is to be asset-based and internally focused, then it will be in very important ways "relationship driven." Thus, one of the central challenges for asset-based community developers is to constantly build and rebuild the relationships between and among local residents, local associations, and local institutions" (Kretzmann, McKnight; 1996).

This level of detail and relationship-centered development is bolstering the strides made in women's lives through Perspectives-Family. It gives them a sense of purpose, a place in the world that is not focused around pain, suffering, and poverty. This asset-based method alters individual outlooks on life because it offers hope and visible change. It tells people "you have something to give, you have something to work for, you have people to love"; it targets the compassion and need for something better we all hold. It builds stronger communities through basic human decency and connection.

Concerning PLACE, the theory of Asset-Based Community Development could be applied to community living. Encouraging the benefits and strengths of each individual in sustainable, transitional housing - such as PLACE - would not only create a strong foundational community but would also become a force of empowerment and a catalyst for growth. Perspectives-Family is hoping to be in charge of providing the assessments and out-treatment programs for women and their children moving into one of the 12 unites PLACE has designated for transitional housing. PLACE is in the process of deciding whether these units will be their own version of supportive housing with the services provided by Perspectives-Family, or if the units will be transitional housing for women and children coming out of Perspectives-Family supportive housing agreements. In any case, the role of Perspectives-Family in empowering mothers and rebuilding families will play an integral role in the development of PLACE. The woman you have pictured, the child she is connected to, will both have an opportunity at a just life filled with increasing opportunity because they were given a chance.

A Little More Perspective (Part II)

PLACE's mission statement includes a just world for all. To better understand, we sat down with Jeannie Seely Smith, CEO of the non-profit Perspectives-Family. She and her organization assist women struggling with homelessness due to a combination of chemical dependency and mental illness (which often go hand in hand). Although she is uncertain of the exact role that Perspectives-Family will have with PLACE in St. Louis Park, she knows that in some way they will come together to change housing for the community for the better.

My research partner, Zoe, and I wandered into Perspectives-Family, not exactly knowing what to expect but feeling extremely grateful that the CEO was available and willing to make time to chat with us. We signed-in and sat in the waiting room that was sprinkled with kids' toys and an artificial fireplace. We were both fairly nervous and felt a little unprepared as we bounced ideas back and forth about our understanding of the non-profit. When another Perspective-Family employee offered us a tour because the CEO was dealing with a crisis, we gratefully accepted.

The building was much larger than either of us had anticipated. There was a kitchen that supplies hot meals and hosts one of their programs called "Kids' Café". One of the rooms for group therapy had a closet full of food options moms could quickly make that their kids would willingly eat: comfort foods like mac and cheese, healthy cereal, and pasta. Another room had the door shut as kids were napping. We saw a classroom full of artwork, an outdoor playground, and a hallway full of offices for mental health professionals, before returning to the administrative part of the building. At the end of the tour, we admitted to each other how impressed we were not only with the space, but the intentionality employees put into what they were doing. We could feel the dedication around us.

We were able to see the theories discussed in our Leadership for Social Justice class come to life. Strategies from the social change wheel were all around us. The programs provide education for mothers and children, teaching new habits and helping to discard any old, toxic ones. To do this, they took away barriers that would otherwise hinder them. An article we read for class, "Assets-based Community Development," by John Kretzmann and John P. McKnight, discussed the importance of building local relationships within neighborhoods for the betterment of the community. This was evident in the work of Perspectives-Family and intersected with the community building strategy of the social change wheel. When we finally got time with Jeannie Seely Smith we were brimming with interest and peppered her with questions about her story, the organization, and PLACE. In 25 minutes we gained insight into her journey, how far Perspectives-Family had come, and possibilities of a growing relationship with PLACE.

Ms. Seeley Smith kind of stumbled into her career at Perspectives, which she has made her home and passion over the last few decades. She started out with a degree in political science and a talent for writing. This contributed to her skill with grant writing and fundraising. In the beginning of her work at Perspectives-Family, the focus was on upscale clients with chemical dependency issues. However, they have transitioned since then, in both clientele and services. First, they entered the prison systems, and focused on stopping the cycle which often leads to women returning as repeat offenders. They were inspired after visiting the prison and also appalled by the conditions women were expected to live in. The superintendent of the time was also committed to creating a more comfortable system for women that could further support them. As they created a program to bring resources to women, they saw a turn around. From there, they realized that to really make change they needed to support women by removing the barriers in front of them.

Today, this is seen in a variety of ways at Perspectives-Family, like the closet-full of food in the group therapy room. If a mother is distracted by what she is going to feed her kids that night, therapy cannot be her focus for the hour she is there. So, Perspectives-Family does what they can and offers food that is realistic to make. These are not the unwanted items from the back of a cupboard but chosen ingredients to make meals that kids will eat. While standing in the classroom filled with art made by children, we were told about how kids go there after school and have time to be quiet, time to themselves, and time to make artwork. They put intention into kids taking care of themselves which in turn helps families. Relationship matters. Perspectives-Family helps foster self-improvement of all types and removes barriers otherwise detrimental to the success of overcoming chemical dependency and addressing mental illness.

From the conversation with Ms. Seeley Smith, we understood that there are a number of potential avenues for how Perspectives-Family will interact with PLACE. Ms. Seeley Smith discussed the possibility of women living in St. Louis Park at PLACE and still having access to Perspectives-Family services. This would be facilitated by two vans running back and forth between the apartments and organization so that kids could still access after school programs and mothers could get to therapy. PLACE would allow them to take on more clients because it would free up other housing options. PLACE would act as the building managers but allow Perspectives-Family to be the landlord. This is necessary because of how Perspectives-Family is run – as a landlord they can evict and will do so if women are not showing up to their mandatory meetings. This would allow Perspectives-Family to grow further and allow them to gain more access to sustainable living options.

In the end, Perspectives and PLACE's relationship is a bit up in the air, but promising. Both organizations want to help address homelessness head-on with supportive or affordable housing. As we left Perspectives-Family, Ms. Seeley Smith led us into a conference room next to where we started across from the artificial fireplace. She showed us framed pictures of the planned extension of the building we were visiting. They hope that legislation for over $4 million in funding will be appropriated by April 2020 to allow the addition of more space for the growing company. She was eager and excited for Perspectives-Family's growth into a bigger building and about their growing relationship with PLACE.

Works Cited:

Perspectives, Inc. (n.d.). Retrieved from https://www.perspectives-family.org/.

Kretzmann, J., & Mcknight, J. P. (1996). Assets-based community development. National Civic Review, 85(4), 23–29. doi: 10.1002/ncr.4100850405

About the Authors:

Zoe Anderson-Miller - I graduated with a double major in Justice and Peace Studies, and Women's Studies. I initially wanted to focus on Perspectives-Family because they were one of the only organizations focused on the experience of women; more specifically a mother and child. This is a relationship I deeply connect with and felt was being celebrated in Perspectives-Family. I hope that by reading this chapter, you recognize the importance of the mother-child relationship; and I hope it gives you a warm feeling to know there are people out there mending relationships and healing families.

Sierra Tentis – Political Science and Justice and Peace Studies with a minor in Public Health were my focus during my time at St. Thomas. Working with PLACE has empowered me to investigate so many of my passions in a real way, and it allowed me to foster a relationship with Perspectives-Family and Jeanie Seeley Smith. This chapter is brought to you with hope, love, and some serious commitment to changing the poverty cycle and institutional structure in which we reside.

A History of Housing in St. Louis Park

Where you live determines access to community assets. Majority white neighborhoods have more parks and more generous tree cover. Communities of color have more environmental hazards like landfills and highways. They have less access to medical care. Schools in these neighborhoods usually have fewer experienced teachers and less challenging curriculum (Mapping Prejudice, 2017). The history of the spaces we inhabit informs much of how they exist today. Where our schools, parks, and public spaces are, what businesses are in our area, even who our neighbors are is a result of unseen history. PLACE's mission, a mixed-income and mixed-use community, seeks to create a diverse community in the heart of St. Louis Park. The future site of PLACE-- 5725 Highway 7-- was initially dedicated to commercial use in 1947.

The plot of land at 5725 was initially purchased to be turned into a Skippy Peanut Butter factory, which by 1977 had become the McGarvey Coffee factory. The coffee factory closed its doors in 2012, and in 2017 the Skippy/ McGarvey building was demolished to make way for the PLACE development which anticipates opening in 2020. But the history of PLACE's site goes beyond just this. A few blocks away from where PLACE will soon open its doors one can find the site of previous racial covenants. To understand the history of where PLACE will soon be, and the history of housing and racial covenants in St. Louis Park, we must look to its larger historical context.

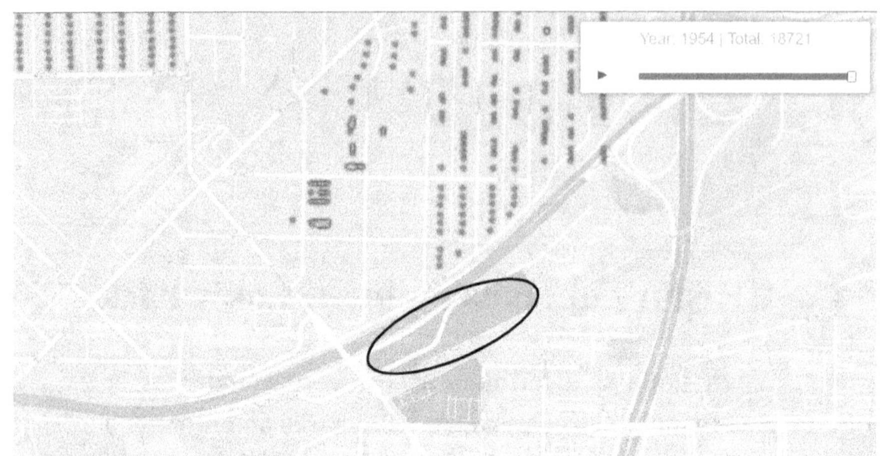

1954: Racial covenants dark gray. Future site of PLACE development circled.

In 1913, as racialized covenants (legally enforceable portions of property deeds that barred non-whites from buying or living on properties), first began to arise in the Twin Cities, St. Louis Park was one of the first places they emerged. The population of St. Louis Park had begun to surge (growing to 1,743 in 1910 while it was only 1,325 a decade earlier), and the village began to invest substantially in public works.

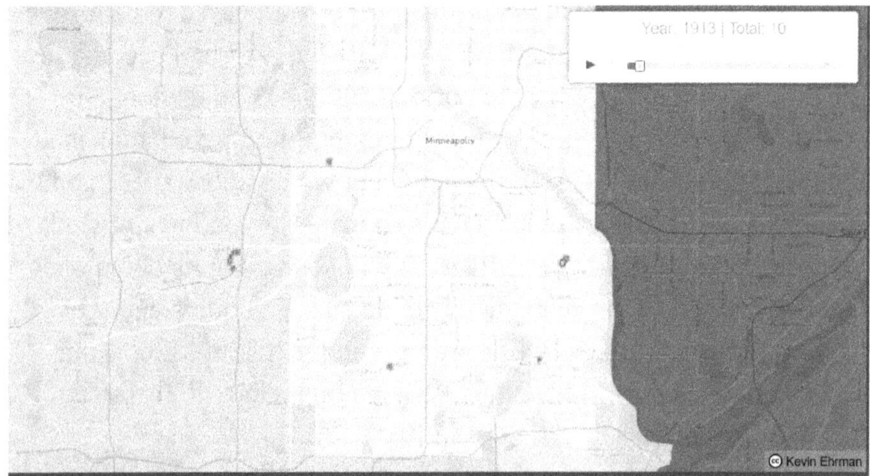

1913: The first racialized covenants emerge in St. Louis Park.

T.B. Walker, the majority landholder in the village, had
previously leased a majority of his St. Louis Park holdings to
factories (such as the Shaft Pierce Shoe Company), but in the 1910's
became "no longer interested in making the village an industrial
center" (Thomas, 1952), instead selling off the thousands of lots of
land he had for sale. Walker began platting-- subdividing-- the land
for private sale. According to the historical society, "the platting...
presaged another attempt to boom the village. Five very fine
qualities which the village could offer were: low taxation, no
municipal debt, two rapid transit lines, industrial trackage, and nine
square miles of space" (Thomas, 1952).

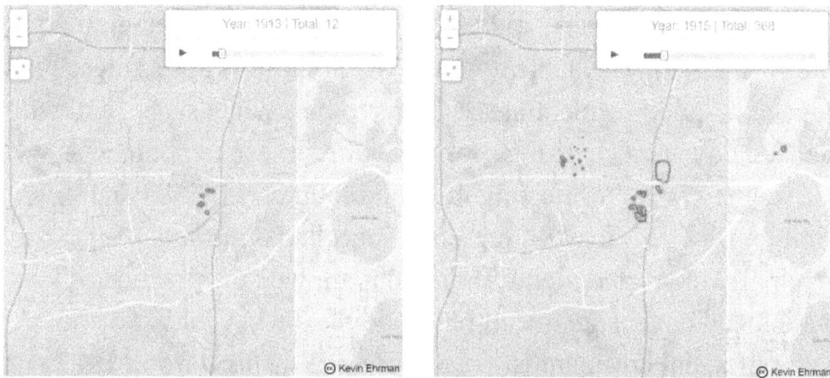

*Racialized covenants in St. Louis Park in 1913 (left) and 1915
(right).*

What the record neglects to show is that these "fine qualities"
were not open to all. Non-whites were purposefully excluded from
living and buying property in St. Louis Park by racialized covenants.
Across the United States around 1915 the number of racial covenants
exploded. The 1915 release of Birth of a Nation depicted African-
Americans as "moronic rapists" and was lauded by the
Superintendent of Minneapolis Public Schools as "the true story of
Reconstruction" (Hatle and Villaincourt, 2009). As St. Louis Park
was platted and thousands of lots were sold to new families and the
village began to transform into a suburb and the population

continued to climb, the number of racial covenants exploded. According to historian Norman Thomas, by 1914 people in St. Louis Park had begun to "think of the village as a place to live-- rather than as being merely a place in which to work... [with] desire to make The Park a good residential area". This shift was reflected in a continued platting of lots, with so much land divided that it indicated "there was an anticipated demand for more lots, or more desirable lots, than were previously platted" (Thomas, 1952).

In 1915, the Minneapolis Journal real estate section was "devoted entirely to telling of the great opportunities in St. Louis Park" (Thomas, 1952) -- the same newspaper that 5 years prior had published an editorial calling for "coordinated action to make neighborhoods all white", and had called race mixing "dangerous" (Delegard, 2019). The subtext was clear; St. Louis Park's future of a village as a "good residential area" was to be a white space, and with racialized covenants backing property values the area boomed as those seeking an all-white neighborhood found St. Louis Park desirable. By 1917, the US Supreme Court had outlawed municipally mandated racial zoning, but allowed the practice of private racial covenants to continue, and the Twin Cities saw the amount of racial covenants increase by more than a third in 1917 alone. In 1919, the Minnesota State Legislature made religion-based covenants illegal, but race-based covenants were allowed to remain on the books.

In 1922, Sam S. Thorpe (the owner of Thorpe Bros Realty) made a purchase of 300 acres of land to be converted into "high-class" subdivisions. In the spring of 1924, 550 lots were put up for sale, all of which were restricted to occupants of "white or caucasian race" (Andersen, 2019). This trend of subtle marketing of "high-class" as whites only continued, and in 1938 the Calhoun Realty advertised a new Knollwood subdivision as "restricted, architecturally controlled subdivision of beautiful picturesque homes", the "restricted" referring to the barring of Jewish and black residents (Andersen, 2019).

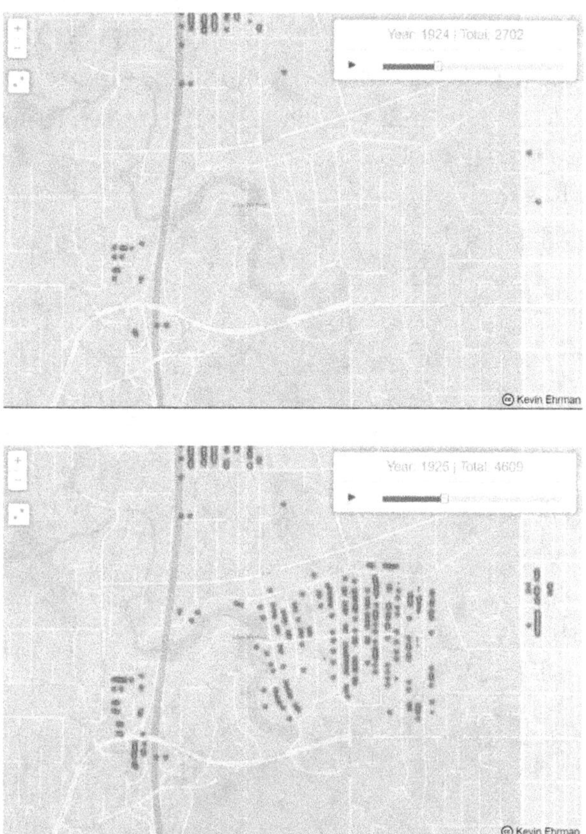

1924 (top) vs. 1925 (bottom): these "high end" developments meant an explosion in racial covenants

Calhoun Realty continued to sell suburban homes, and by 1939 experienced a home sale boom thanks to the Federal Housing Administration (FHA) insuring private mortgages, and this FHA insurance made mortgages much more affordable for families; with notable exceptions. To become eligible for FHA securitization, properties had to meet certain appraisal standards, including racial exclusivity. To ensure eligibility for FHA-backed mortgages, many developers began to apply "proactive" racial covenants. Thus, while the FHA decreased the barriers to white homeownership, it increased the barriers to black homeownership. According to the FHA's 1935 manual, "A change in social or racial occupancy generally leads to an instability and a reduction in value". This language remained on FHA books until 1947, and the FHA mortgage program led to a deep gap in homeownership and wealth rates between white and black communities (Welsh, 2018).

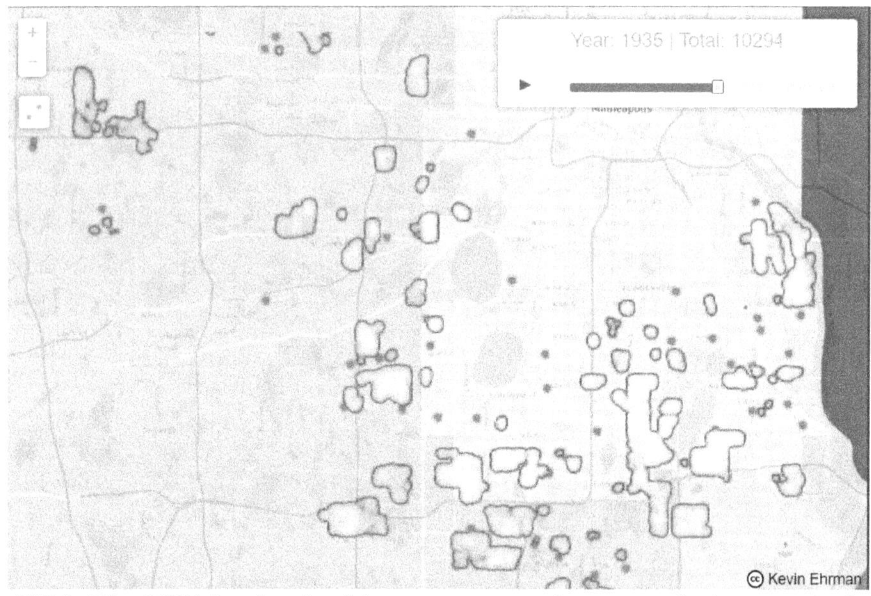

1935: The FHA begins backing mortgages that meet their appraisal criteria (one of which is racial homogeneity), further incentivizing covenants. Racial covenant prevalence explodes in suburbs, and the number of Minneapolis-area covenants surpasses 10,000.

Due to the drastic increase in home affordability and following the return of WWII soldiers, St. Louis Park saw its population increase from around 7,700 in 1940 to over 22,000 in 1950 (Thomas, 1952). In 1948, the Shelley v. Kraemer Supreme Court decision ruled racial covenants were legally unenforceable and a violation of the 14th amendment (Silva, 2009). This ruling, however, did not make covenants illegal or privately unenforceable,

40

and so despite the ruling the covenants remained and continued to bar black and minority families from communities like St. Louis Park.

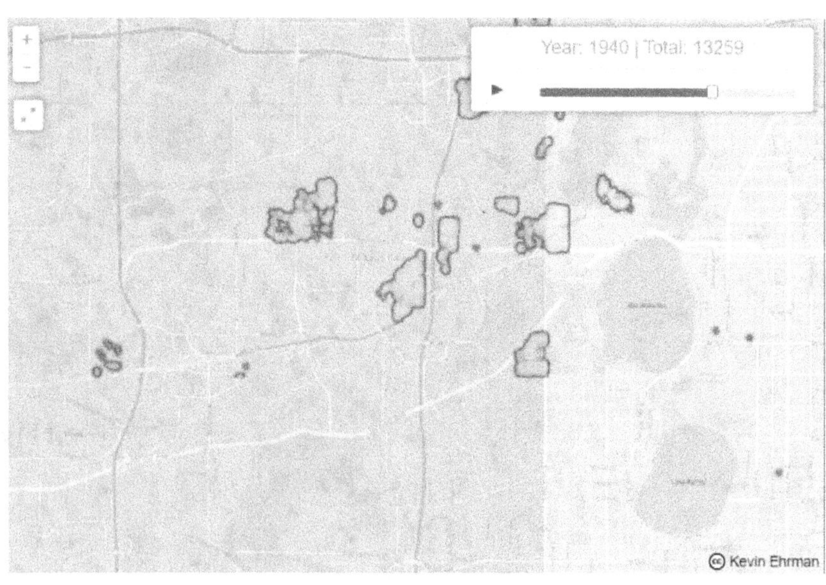

1940 (top) vs. 1950 (bottom): as the population and housing demand in St. Louis Park grows, as do the number of covenants.

With covenants no longer legally enforceable, white families upped their "social enforcement" of these covenants. In 1952, the Lewis family became the first black family to move into St. Louis Park. The family moved into a two-bedroom bungalow at 2928 Jersey Avenue, an area surrounded by homes still under covenants.

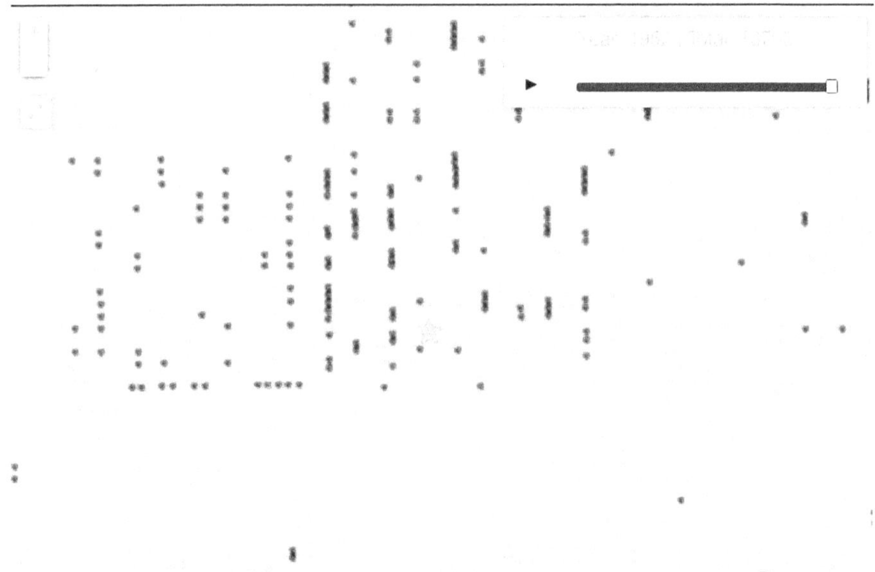

1952: The site of the Lewis family home (star) with homes under covenant in dark gray. The Lewis family was the first black family to move to St. Louis Park.

The landlady, after checking to make sure that neighbors would not have any "objections", rented the home to the Lewis family. However, within days of the family moving in, the landlady drew up an eviction notice, purporting that she had been called by people in the neighborhood that were pressuring her to drive out the family (Thomas, 1952). The family, allowed to spend only 6 months in St. Louis Park, soon after moved to Minneapolis. Even though there was no longer legally enforceable covenants to prevent minority families from moving to St. Louis Park, social pressure acted to enforce segregation and tenants could still be evicted based on their race due to the lack of housing protections.

It was not until 1968 and the passage of the Fair Housing Act that racial covenants finally became illegal, and the act prohibited "discrimination of sale, rental, and financing of dwellings and other housing-related transactions, based on race, color, national origin, religion, [and] sex" (Silva, 2009). Even still, many racial covenants remain in the fine print of deeds; an ugly reminder of the way that neighborhoods were purposefully racially constructed. While now illegal, the legacy of these covenants and their consequences persists. Today, the Twin Cities have the lowest rate of African-American home-ownership in the country (Delegard, 2019).

Works Cited

Andersen, J. (2019). The Brookside Timeline. Retrieved from
        https://twincitiesmusichighlights.net/timeline/.

Delegard, K. (2019). Racial Housing Covenants in the Twin Cities.
        Retrieved from https://www.mnopedia.org/thing/racial-
        housing-covenants-twin-cities.

Hatle, E. D., & Vaillancourt, N. M. (2009). One Flag, One School,
        One Language: Minnesota's Ku Klux Klan in the 1920s.
        Minnesota Historical Society.

Mapping Prejudice. (2017). Retrieved from
        https://www.mappingprejudice.org/what-
        arecovenants/index.html.

Silva, C. (2009). Racial Restrictive Covenants History: Enforcing
        neighborhood segregation in Seattle. Retrieved from
        https://depts.washington.edu/civilr/covenants_report.htm.

Thomas, N. (1952). Chapter IX: The War and Changing Attitudes
        about the Village, 1914-1920. Retrieved from
        http://slphistory.org/nt-ix/.

Welsh, Nancy H. (2018). "Racially Restrictive Covenants in the United States: A Call to Action," Agora Journal of Urban Planning and Design, 130-142.

Citation for images:

Ehrman, K. (2019). All images retrieved from Mapping Prejudice website: https://www.mappingprejudice.org/index.html

About the Author – Maddy Flisk

As a Biology major at the University of St. Thomas, I have been increasingly involved in ecology and health, and how personal health and wellbeing depends on identity. My hometown neighborhood in Chicago was constructed through redlining and blockbusting, the scars of which are omnipresent in the city today. Today, I am a route manager for Brightside Produce, a produce distribution program that seeks to increase access to produce in food-insecure communities.

Racialized Housing Covenants

As we strive to create a better world, it is of paramount need to address harmful policies and practices by confronting past injustices that caused great harm and inequity to African American communities as well as other people of color and immigrants. Structural racism benefits white people at the expense of people of color.

Historical policies and practices are one way of understanding structural racism in the US. "Structural Racism in the U.S. is the normalization and legitimization of an array of dynamics – historical, cultural, institutional and interpersonal – that routinely advantage whites while producing cumulative and chronic adverse outcomes for people of color" (Lawrence, 2004) Specifically looking at redlining and housing covenants, the magnitude of the effects of structural racism details the outcomes of these policies.

I sat down with Kevin Ehrman-Solberg, one of the co-founders of the Mapping Prejudice Project. Mapping Prejudice is a research project that shows structural barriers that prevented African Americans and other people of color from buying and renting property by mapping housing covenants in Minneapolis. Mapping prejudice aims to uncover and communicate the impact of racialized housing covenants by showing how covenants shaped the city of Minneapolis as well as racial disparities. "Racial restrictive covenants - private agreements barring non-Caucasians from occupying or owning property -were a key element of the

segregationist policies in the early twentieth-century United States."
(Weaver, 1944)

Kevin Ehrman-Solberg has profound insights to offer on the role of racialized housing covenants in the development of Minneapolis and in relation to current inequities. He says, "Covenants have a material impact on wealth and this is one of the things that we are grappling with this project. This isn't just about racism as an ideology or as a value system, or personal preference, this is racism that produces material, measurable, quantifiable, economic benefit to white people at the expense of people of color.

Intergenerational transfer of wealth

According to Kevin, "Covenants weren't just an indicator of bias, covenants have a material impact on wealth. We've done some work on redlining too and the inverse is also true so covenanted homes over-perform city median today and what that means is a covenanted home is worth significantly more, about 14% than the standard value of a house in Minneapolis. Homes in redlined areas are under-performing city median value by about 25%. So that means, essentially, it's about a one hundred thousand dollar difference. So, if your parents were white and were able to buy a house in a covenanted neighborhood, you have accumulated about a hundred grand in additional wealth that somebody who's grandparents who weren't white and bought a home in a redlined neighborhood would have today."

Policies and homeownership between black and white people

Kevin speaks about the economic impact of covenants that are still prevalent today. "That particular mechanism has been illegal since the Fair Housing Act of 1968 but the economic impacts of racial covenants are still very much with us today and can be seen in the contemporary disparities between black and white homeownership in Minneapolis which is actually the worst in the country; of the 102 largest metro areas in the United States,

46

Minneapolis has the largest gap between black and white homeownership rates (Metrostats, 2016) at about 50%. About 75% of white families own their home in the city and only about 25% of black families own their home in the city. and we think covenants help us understand how that came to be. A gap of that significance doesn't just happen, it takes a lot of work to produce those conditions and now that we have this comprehensive database of covenants we are able to figure out some of these causal relationships and linkages between historic practices and policies and contemporary racial disparity." (Kevin Ehrman-Solberg)

How covenants shaped contemporary cities

Kevin Erhman Solberg talks about how the underlying effects of covenants can be seen in contemporary cities and Mapping Prejudice's community-based approach. "The number of connections people have made by looking at or interacting with this spatial dataset is mind- boggling, we have folks look at this map and go 'oh that actually correlates almost exactly with where urban tree canopy is highest or lowest, somebody saw our map and said this explains why certain streets have trees planted on them and others don't and I never would've made that connection."

"The normal story of covenants is that people of color, African Americans specifically moved into white neighborhoods, white neighborhoods freaked out so they erected racial covenants as a barrier, so its framed as this very reactive thing. In Minneapolis however, covenants go into places before anybody even lives there, it's much more of this forward thinking, forward planning tool rather than a reactive one. Almost all the covenants are put in place by developers, we see covenants kind of appear, at least in the legal record on land before that land even has houses on it, before roads have been extended to that part of town, the people putting covenants in weren't thinking about right now, they were thinking 50 years out, they were thinking 20, 100 years out. What that's done is that this kind of intentionally racialized landscape determined how the city was going to get built out and who was gonna be able to live where, it determined subsequent decisions on investments, like where do parks go for example, we found that connects very closely with racial covenants. The inverse of course is also true, where freeways go this connects directly with areas that were redlined. "You'd almost be hardpressed to find something in the city that doesn't connect in some meaningful way with this historical era of racial covenants."

Restitution

"We all have a political commitment to restorative justice and restitution and reparation. I view our role more as facilitative, we can arm communities with data, we can use resources at the U and the expertise we have to build these datasets and build these maps and get that information out there, we can use our position to elevate other voices.

> a.) "data project and we need more data to figure out how stuff work better
>
> b.) it's about changing the narrative, changing popular understandings of how racial inequality was formed and reproduced in Minneapolis and I feel like that's the place where we can best do work." (Kevin Ehrman-Solberg)

Emotional labor on people of color

Kevin believes that the Mapping Prejudice project "can be valuable and support this larger project of reparations and restitution without colonizing the project."

On what he wrestles with: "one thing that I am increasingly convinced is vital is intentionally adopting an iterative approach to both the framing of the questions you're asking and the methods of research that you are employing and what I mean by that is that normally how funding works is that I come up with my idea, I apply for funding, I get my grant and map out exactly what I'm going to do and write something about it at the end of it and there is very little room in that model to react to things and alter trajectories and With Mapping Prejudice initially our plan was to find a few covenants, we were just gonna do a sample, write an article about it and that was gonna be it but right out of the gate we also decided that as we're doing this we want to be talking to people about it. We don't just want be hanging out in archives and talking amongst ourselves.

Right away we got all these community responses and reactions that made us fundamentally rethink what we were doing, what the scope of our project should be, what the value of our work was. One of the earliest discoveries, I guess you could call it is that representative work like that doesn't do as much as when you allow people to place themselves in the geography of racial covenants." Mapping Prejudice is a project that aims to uncover and communicate the impact of racialized housing covenants by showing how covenants shaped the city of Minneapolis as well as racial disparities. "Racial restrictive covenants - private agreements barring non-Caucasians from occupying or owning property were a key element of the segregationist policies in the early twentieth-century United States." (Jones-Correa, 2000, p. 541) "Minneapolis isn't much of a city before 1900." says Kevin Ehrman-Solberg, one of the co-founders of the Mapping Prejudice Project. "there aren't that many people here, the expansion of this Minneapolis city coincides almost exactly with the use and deployment of racial covenants, so of course if a city's boom period is also the period when you can just racially restrict entire neighborhoods that's going to impact the way the city gets built out and the way the city looks."
Initially, the Mapping Prejudice team did not anticipate the project to be this big, but once they opened it up and got involved with communities, they saw the role they could play to help tell the story of the seriousness of structural racism.

"For me what I want out of this project is for white people to take structural racism seriously, at the end of the day and I want white people to situate themselves in these material legacies of white supremacy that were made material through things like racial covenants." (Kevin Ehrman Solberg)

Though housing covenants and redlining are illegal today, they still continue to impact minority communities. "Home ownership is without question the single most important means of accumulating Lassets" and thus increasing wealth." One of the explanations for the enormous racial inequality in terms of wealth is directly attributable to mortgage lending discrimination. In particular, the historical practice of racial redlining has foreclosed the opportunity of homeownership to vast numbers of African-Americans." (Nier III, 1998, p. 617)

A recurring theme in this topic and interview for me is the responsibility that is upon us to address these past injustices and that is exactly what Mapping Prejudice is doing. Kevin Ehrman-Solberg's story of us looks at housing as a larger issue that is connected to the wellbeing of us as a whole. He talked about how structural racism is "baked into the fabric of Minneapolis" and that we collectively have to do something with this knowledge that is not new to people of color and that we "have to confront and acknowledge the legacy of racial covenants and redlining, really a history that has been intentionally forgotten." Acknowledging this history is an essential first step if we are to do things right in the future, the task at hand is not only working for a more just and equal community but to accept the history as well as restitution for the communities that were harmed as a result.

Works Cited:

Metrostats (2016). Retrieved from:
        https://metrocouncil.org/getdoc/03bd679d-21a4-455b-af7a-
        15309b0c71ae/Diving-Deeper-Understanding-Disparities-
        Between-B.aspx)

About the author - Laila Sheikh

I am international student from Nairobi, Kenya and I come from a big, loving family. I am pursuing degrees in Geographic Information Systems and Environmental Studies at the University of St. Thomas. I hope to one day start a non-profit organization in Kenya that addresses public health concerns to help my community.

PLACE

Bringing Success to St. Louis Park

St. Louis Park consists of thirty-four different neighborhoods. It was established in 1890 for the purpose of industrial work with residential communities to ensure close and easy access to their workplace. This community was not built to be cohesive, due to the layout the industrial offices interrupt the residential areas but that didn't stop the communities from growing and expanding. The location of this community is minutes away from Minneapolis and continues to expand today through growing populations and transit opportunities. A new addition to this community is People Linking Artists, Community, and Environment (PLACE). PLACE is co-operating with the City of St. Louis Park to create a mixed-income, transit-oriented community focused on sustainable living. The addition of PLACE will be an incredibly positive influence on the community of St. Louis Park and will unite the community in a way it has never experienced.

This organization has an original location, WAV in Ventura, California. It has been an incredible success and has had a huge impact on the community it resides in. It is home to over 50 residential artists and is a new kind of community, an arts eco-village. The apartments are "powered by the sun, built from recycled and sustainable materials, and designed to use a fraction of the water consumed in conventional buildings. WAV is the greenest community ever built in Ventura, and the first sustainable arts community in the world." The success this organization had in

Ventura is creating hope for the community in St. Louis Park, Minnesota. St. Louis Park is incredibly excited to host this new community due to its five-year goal plan as they, "Seek opportunities to improve the environmental design and energy efficiencies of our properties. Utilize energy-saving and environmentally friendly equipment, appliances and building technique and products". PLACE isn't the first residential building with sustainability in mind, in Minneapolis, New Construction and Substantial Renovation has had a huge impact and success by building homes with planned developments and sustainable infrastructure. This development doesn't extend it's hand as far as PLACE does within sustainability but found great success with energy, resource, and water conservation. Many people worry PLACE and other communities like it will change the community from what it is now and face gentrification challenges. PLACE doesn't see themselves as motivators of gentrification because they believe in small and local businesses while supporting small artists. John Bardi a resident of WAV in Ventura, California. John believes, "WAV was good for the area and the beginning of a renaissance. The changes were subtle, it's difficult to move to an equitable world. WAV opens the door for change". With buildings going up in St. Louis Park, the community can expect the best attempt at an equitable society.

Despite the changes PLACE will bring to St. Louis Park, it is believed this community is ready to face the changes and wants the sustainable options in their community. Minnesota has taken a leap into the future of sustainable living in America. PLACE opens the doors and options for people of all incomes, races, and genders. John Bardi believes that "Places like WAV are the future and the only options America will have in the future as we continue to face the challenges of progressing society … I couldn't be happier. I feel that I do good work where I live and we (all of the residents) bring all of our skills to contribute to the community we live in". The positivity of this organization is contagious and will leave less than a carbon footprint but will definitely progress the community for to a more just society.

57

About the Author - Genevieve Thompson

I am finishing my undergraduate degree at the University of St. Thomas in Justice and Peace Studies as well as History. I look forward to applying to Law schools and hope to stay in the Twin Cities area.

A PLACE to Live

Prefatory Notes

PLACE: Which stands for "Projects Linking Art, Community, and Environment", is an organization which collaborates with cities to design and build vibrant places for people to live and work. PLACE is currently developing a mixed-income housing complex in St. Louis Park, Minnesota.

This chapter is by no means intended as an editorial. Nor is it an effort to display conclusions, positive or negative, about St. Louis Park, PLACE, or any other mixed housing complex. It is purely a reporting of (1) an in-progress development of a mixed housing complex, and (2) a unique, insider perspective of PLACE and the overall dynamics of affordable housing coming from one of the six PLACE team members, Todd Bagby, affiliated with this project. The rest of the team members represent an eclectic group. Their backgrounds consist of (but are not limited to) law, urban planning, architecture, and civic engagement.

I am an emerging scholar hailing from the University of St. Thomas, currently learning the nuances of qualitative research. This project was birthed from my Leadership for Justice and Peace class, with faculty mentor and instructor Mike Klein. Initially, I wanted to focus on how the law intersected with affordable housing. This changed however, once I began recording his answers to the first couple of questions. I had to rethink how I asked my questions. I started asking idiomatic questions in addition to academic ones to solicit more conversational responses. The interview then allowed me to change my focus from the law and drove me in the direction of the dynamics of affordable housing and affordable living.

The following interview was conducted at Todd's temporary office in downtown Minneapolis in an open space where affiliates of the complex would occasionally roam. A classmate of mine, Joshua Crespo, assisted in asking the questions. Additionally, my computer did quite an impressive job of picking up most of the conversation. As a disclaimer, there were times when the audio would not pick up certain phrases or words, thus, forcing me to add brackets to words that were slightly unclear. Despite this seeming like a setback, it was only a minor hinderance and the meaning stayed clear.

Todd is unique in his own right. Affordable housing is expressed through his eyes. Whether his sentiments are the archetype of affordable housing or open to criticism is up to the judgement of the reader, looking at this issue through their individual experiences, second-hand sources and self-reflection.

Finally, there are two theoretical concepts that will be addressed in the transcription. They will be used to substantiate Todd's responses and provide a social context to this chapter.

1.   Story of Self/Us/Now by Marshall Ganz: "Social movement leaders tell new public stories: a story of self, a story of us, and a story of now. A story of self-communicates the values that call one to action. A story of us communicates the values shared by those in action. A story of now communicates an urgent challenge to those values that demands action now."

2.   Asset-Based Community Development by John Kretzmann and John McKnight "Asset-based community development (Kretzmann & McKnight, 1993), a particular approach to community building, assumes that social and economic revitalization starts with what is already present within a community - not only the capacities of residents as individuals, but also the existing

commercial, associational and institutional foundation. This involves pinpointing, or "mapping," all of the available assets in the community, and connecting, or "mobilizing," them in ways that multiply their power and effectiveness. An asset-based approach to community building perceives local residents and other community stakeholders as active change agents rather than passive beneficiaries or clients." (Turner and Pinkett, 2000, pg. 1)

A Demographic Overview and Brief Synopsis of Housing in St. Louis Park

Population

The Village of St. Louis Park was founded in 1886. There were two landowners and five businessmen from Minneapolis who created the St. Louis Park Land and Improvement Company. This was officially the city's first developer. Between the years of 1886 and 1887, they platted three subdivisions, which included commercial, residential, and industrial.

By 1890, the population of St. Louis Park was 499. In this year, Thomas Barlow Walker, a business magnate and art collector, noticed the uptick in the population and developed the Village into a commercial, industrial, and residential area. This began to create a sense of community. The second noticeable population increase occurred shortly after World War II, with a population count of 22,644 by 1950. Because of this trend, St. Louis Park was crowned as a city by an overwhelming majority vote of its residents who approved a home rule charter in 1954. Once 1970 rolled around, the population plateaued at 48,883 (United States Census Bureau, 2014). As of 2017, the population was 49,029 people. (United States Census Bureau, 2017)

Senior Housing and Affordable Subsidized Senior Housing

Senior housing development refers to any housing development that is restricted to people age 55 or older. (Maxfield Consulting, 2018). In St. Louis Park, there are five different types of senior living environments:

1. Adult/Few Services; where few, if any, support services are provided, and rents tend to be modest as a result;
2. Congregate/Optional-Services; where support services such as meals and light housekeeping are available for an additional fee;
3. Congregate/Service-Intensive; where support services such as meals and light housekeeping are included in the monthly rents;
4. Assisted Living; where two or three daily meals as well as basic support services such as transportation, housekeeping and/or linen changes are included in the fees. Personal care services such as assistance with bathing, grooming and dressing is included in the fees or is available either for an additional fee or included in the rents.
5. Memory Care; where more rigorous and service-intensive personal care is required for people with dementia and Alzheimer's disease. Typically, support services and meal plans are like those found at assisted living facilities, but the heightened levels of personalized care demand more staffing and higher rental fees.

Planned and Proposed Housing Developments

Understanding the multi-housing development structure will assist in providing context to the interview. The data was compiled by the city of St. Louis Park and Maxfield Consulting (2018). PLACE is located at the bottom of this graph.

TABLE P-1
MULTI-HOUSING DEVELOPMENT PIPELINE
CITY OF ST. LOUIS PARK
2010 - March 2018

Project Name/Address	Developer	Project Occupancy	MR	AFF	Total Units	Project Type
Recently Completed						
The Shoreham 3907 Highway 7	Bader Development	Opened May 2017	118	30	148	Mixed-use/ Mixed-income
4800 Excelsior 4760 and 4800 Excelsior Blvd	Weidner Apartment Homes	Opened December 2017	146	18	164	Mixed-use/ Mixed-income/ General-Occupancy
Central Park West Apartments- Phase I I-394 and Highway 100	DLC Residential	Opened 2017	199	6	198	General-Occupancy
Millenium at West End Apartments 1600 West End Blvd	DLC Residential	Opened October 2015	158	0	158	General-Occupancy
Siena Apartment Homes 6800 Cedar Lake Rd	Eliot Park Apartments, LLC	Opened September 2015	138	0	138	General-Occupancy
e2 (Ellipse on Excelsior II) 3924 Excelsior Blvd	Bader Development	Opened August 2013	58	0	58	General-Occupancy
Hoigaard Village-The Adagio 3690 36th St W	Dunbar Development	Opened 2013	100	0	100	General-Occupancy
The Flats at West End 5310 16th St W	Dolce Lving	Opened 2013	119	0	119	General-Occupancy
Verge Park Center Blvd & 36th St	E.J. Plesko and Associates & SilverCrest	Opened 2013	192	0	192	General-Occupancy
The Ellipse on Excelsior 3920 Excelsior Blvd	Bader Development	Opened September 2010	132	0	132	General-Occupancy
Under Construction						
Parkway 25 4001 County Road 25 and 4025 Highway 7	Paz Sela, Sela Investments	Construction began in Fall 2017	112	0	112	Mixed-use/ General Occupancy
The Elmwood 5606 W. 36th St.	Main Street Company	Spring 2019	53	17	70	Senior, Mixed-income
Approved						
Arlington Row- East & West 7700 Block of Wayzata Blvd & Southwest corner of Wayzata Blvd and Texas Ave	Melrose Company	On-Hold	61	0	61	General-Occupancy
Central Park East Apartments- Phase II I-394 and Highway 100	DLC Residential	N/A	153	11	164	Mixed-Income
Platia Place 9920 Wayzata Blvd	Stoddard Companies	Fall 2019	122	27	149	Mixed-income; 122-key limited service hotel
Via SE quadrant of Hwy 7 and Wooddale Ave	PLACE (Projects, Linking Art, Community & Environment)		99	200	299	Mixed-use/ Mixed-income; 2 buildings, 99 artists' apartments
Proposed						
RFP - Beltline LRT stop	Sherman Group	TBD: June 2019?	192	48	240	Mixed-income

Sources: City of St. Louis Park, Maxfield Research & Consulting, LLC

Source, Maxwell Research and Consulting, LLC; City of St. Louis Park, 2018, p. 144

Demographic Profile and Housing Demand

PLACE, as a mixed-income, affordable housing complex, will be providing shelter to various groups shown in the table below.

Entry-level householders	**First-time homebuyers and move-up renters**	**Move-up homebuyers**
• Often prefer to rent basic, inexpensive apartments • Usually singles or couples in their early 20's without children • Will often "double-up" with roommates in apartment setting	• Often prefer to purchase modestly-priced single-family homes or rent more upscale apartments • Usually married or cohabiting couples, in their mid-20's or 30's, some with children, but most are without children	• Typically prefer to purchase newer, larger, and therefore more expensive single-family homes • Typically, families with children where householders are in their late 30's to 40's

Empty-nesters (persons whose children have grown and left home) and never-nesters (persons who never have children)	Younger independent Seniors	Older seniors
• Prefer owning but will consider renting their housing • Some will move to alternative lower-maintenance housing products • Generally, couples in their 50's or 60's	• Prefer owning but will consider renting their housing • Often move (at least part of the year) to retirement havens in the Sunbelt and desire to reduce their responsibilities for upkeep and maintenance • Generally, in their late 60's or 70's	• May need to move out of their single-family home due to physical and/or health constraints or a desire to reduce their responsibilities for upkeep and maintenance • Generally single females (widows) in their mid-70's or older

Source, Maxwell Research and Consulting, 2018, p. 145

2040 Comprehensive Plan

Over the past several years, the city of St. Louis Park has taken an initiative to improve the quality of life for its residents. The 2040 Comprehensive Plan "includes key community elements that set forth the future direction of the city. Certain elements are required to be addressed by State law, including land use, transportation, housing, surface water management, public facilities, and capital improvements." (2040 Comprehensive Plan St. Louis Park, Minnesota, August 2019, p. 8) These elements are included in the transcription below and are represented in the PLACE development.

Todd Bagby

Biography: Todd Bagby has dedicated his life to housing and community development. He is a law, planning, and development professional who works with local groups, governments, and various design, construction, finance, and other professionals to create vibrant, innovative, and sustainable communities. With over 15 years of combined experience in law and community development, he is skilled in building alliances, leveraging efficiencies, and navigating obstacles to accomplish great things with limited resources.

Todd has helped obtain funding for and optimize the usability and accessibility of an adaptive reuse project involving a former casket factory. He has counseled and represented local governments, conducted multimillion-dollar litigation, represented children in foster care, and helped enforce ADA regulations as part of the U.S. Department of Justice.

Todd is a licensed attorney in Minnesota and Colorado (inactive) and an AICP Candidate, serving on the Equity and Diversity Committee of the Minnesota Chapter of the American Planning Association. Todd has a Bachelor of Science degree from Tulane University and Master of Science and Juris Doctor degrees from the University of Iowa, where Todd received the Jim Harris Memorial Award for his commitment to community.
In his spare time, Todd coaches youth basketball and teaches language arts (and occasionally math) at Summit Academy OIC. He is also an artist of sorts, having produced works as a musician, filmmaker, and podcaster.

Interview

Martin: What is your interest in housing? Additionally, after working in the legal field, what made you want to get back to pursue your master's degree in urban planning?

Todd: So, something that's interesting about housing is that there's a tangible product. I mean, that's not the biggest thing, but it's nice to have something to look at afterwards, right? I can say, "So that is part of what my hard work went in to." Also, housing touches people on a very fundamental level. There's been studies that show that security around housing is the most fundamental thing someone can possess. If you have a secure place to live and you're not going from couch to couch on a given night, that's going to make more of an impact on your life positively than anything else that anybody else could possibly do for you. It's aspects of accessibility. A lot of the built environment overlooks people with different abilities, and you can't imagine what that could be like for them. I mean, if you don't have a disability of any sort, it's hard to relate to how the built environment doesn't serve somebody with different abilities until you talk to somebody with different abilities. That was a lot of experience that I had early on. I developed an appreciation for how housing touches people's lives and just how important it is.

Josh: We all have privileges and we all have certain advantages in this life. For me personally, I don't need to think about how I am going to enter a building or apartment complex since I have legs that will allow me to do so. I don't have to consciously think, "Hmm… what are alternative ways that I can enter said building?" So, my experiences are different than someone who is wheelchair bound. How are your experiences different than those who may not be as well off? How does this relate to your efforts for PLACE?

Todd: Anything I can claim to know about anything comes from talking with folks that may have disabilities. They may have stories to tell about experiences where they found themselves in a wheelchair and came to the realization that they were unable to traverse the street. It's hard for me to imagine. I think that my privileges are drastically different, and I think that's something that I must always challenge myself to recognize. I try to do that by talking to my fellow humans around me. We all have something different going on. In some of my experiences, I worked with the kids at Tanager Place and at a bureaucratic, governmental level at the Department of Justice (DOJ). An interesting experience I had at the Department of Justice was to focus on year-old complaints of cruise lines. People on cruise lines have run into a lot of problems. There was one example where we had a case file full of complaints that had been written about certain cruise lines. When I was an intern working at the Department of Justice, I opened up some of these case files. One was a letter from a mother talking about how her family had saved up a lot of money to take a trip on a cruise. Her child had Type 1 Diabetes. The family had tried to make arrangements beforehand to make sure that the insulin would be available and refrigerated for the trip. That way they could enjoy the cruise and have a pleasant family vacation. They thought that everything was arranged, but a lot of things were overlooked, and then during their trip they had a situation where the child had a medical emergency. It was a traumatic experience for the family. They didn't have a lot of money to put together for vacations. This (incident) had a severe impact on the family. I ended up following up on this case, which was five years after [the complaint] was written, and I ended up contacting the mother. I interviewed her and asked her about the fact pattern behind the case to see whether it might be something that the Department of Justice could potentially reinforce and get involved in. This simple gesture brought her to tears. Even though it was five years later, which I think is horrible that a response had to come from an intern five years later, but having any access or response whatsoever was important to me, and she was happy that the issue hadn't fallen on deaf ears. So, in conclusion, understanding how my experiences differ from someone else comes from meeting and listening to what people have to say. It is important that we (PLACE) get out there and find experiences like this. I wasn't there for this, but for the WAV development, the staff conducted 137 community engagement events. So, going out, talking to folks and ask them questions like, "what are you trying to accomplish here?" and "what input can you provide us that we can use to help you?" is crucial. It is paramount that you do not make decisions for communities. You want to make sure that they play a part in the development of their community. We (representatives of PLACE) want to make sure to do the best we can to ensure that we are checking in with folks and learning things about them that will be important for us as we move forward with the development of PLACE.

Martin: So far Josh and I have learned that you have devoted a wholesome amount of time on housing-related issues. You have looked at housing through the lens of academia, policy, law and maybe some other areas that we may not have touched on yet. After looking at it through all these different perspectives, how would you define housing?

Todd: I would define housing as secure and stable shelter. So it's a home, you know, and I think it's easy to get sort of cold when you look at things through an academic lens or from a developer's perspective. (From a developer's perspective) their looking at a lot of numbers and thinking, "We would like to create this many units, or we'll need this many tax credits or these many bonds to make this happen" and so forth. It can be easy to get cold about it. But when it comes down to it it's people's homes. And Chris Velasco, our executive director, is very good about reminding us what our true mission is all about and as an organization we are very proud that a lot of the people that move into our developments are able and decide to stay there. It's not just transitional housing. You know the WAV development that we opened in 2009? Well a lot of people that moved in on that first day are still there. And there is a section of WAV that is transitional housing that is geared specifically for the homeless. So, the transitional housing is a program that is designed to bring people out of homelessness, but a number of those people that have gotten out of that transitional housing have transitioned into permanent housing. So, I mean those are things that we are really proud of, and we always try to keep in mind. We have to remember that these are people's homes.

Josh: What do you appreciate and believe about affordable housing?

Todd: Affordable housing is really interesting in the context of other social dynamics. Like we talked about, housing is a fundamental aspect to people's lives. If you look at Maslow's Hierarchy of Needs, shelter is right there at the bottom of the pyramid. It's one of the fundamental points. And in the same vein housing is a primary part of society. Now there's residential neighborhoods in which people live in houses or multi-family apartments. Affordable housing has this interesting history of stigma attached to it. Anytime you propose to add affordable housing to any part of town, you're going to have folks who will immediately start thinking of the "other" as coming into the neighborhood, you know what I mean? You may have folks who have lived in a house for 25 years and next door to them all they've known was the vacant Skippy Peanut Butter factory. And that was just fine by them. It didn't bother them. That's just the old peanut butter factory. Now there's been talk that we have got some potential housing that's coming in and it's affordable housing. Sometimes when they hear the word "affordable", it freaks them out. Housing and particularly affordable housing is interesting because it's a primary part of the social dynamic, and people really organize themselves around housing. You could hear comments like, "the "others" may be shopping or living there, so let's not go there". It's like their thinking there's no way developers should build a shopping mall in this area because they wouldn't find it a desirable place to shop. Well, that is where we're going to try to make those connections.

Josh: Has PLACE conducted any research on the history of the area in which their building in? Have they looked at the history of segregation, or the history of homelessness or anything like that around the area?

Todd: I don't think St. Louis Park is special in terms of being a suburb that needs a space for affordable housing. Affordable housing is a drastic need everywhere. Over time, lots of folks have moved out towards the suburbs because of the large influx of jobs in these areas. So affordable housing is becoming a necessity for people. The installation of the light rail will help with that too. St. Louis Park has a really interesting history. It's got a very progressive city council. I think that collaboration with the city could be beneficial, because (in general) many nonprofits don't have large sums of money in the bank. So, if you want to make these projects happen, you've got to have good partners and collaborators. I think we have that with St. Louis Park.

Martin: You have previously talked about projects your working on that focus on mixed income housing. So, relating from that experience and any other prior experience that you've had, also incorporating your experience of seeing the development of PLACE from the beginning and watching it become a housing property, what ways do you believe that the law has played a role as the building blocks of PLACE?

Todd: In terms of the creation of PLACE or the previous housing development project?

Martin: Both.

Todd: So much of what I do is law-related, especially in the affordable housing realm. It's all dictated and carved out by the law, for better or worse. It's great that there are laws that provide public financing and funding to build affordable housing. The way the laws are written are ham-handed sometimes. So, one example is part of the way that affordable housing is defined: It is its own rabbit hole. Basically, how it works is the federal government will say if you spend more than 30% of your personal or household income on housing for your rent payment or mortgage payment, they will continue to be housing burdened. What they do to determine what affordable is, is they look at a given area and take the median income. So, the person with the middle income will have a certain percentage and this will determine what the area median income is. Then there's different levels of affordability based on that so low income. There are multiple levels: 30% of area median income, 50% of area median income, then there's 80% which is considered more like workforce housing. For an example, think of Silicon Valley. What's the area median income? Let's say it's $3 million. A person in the middle makes $3 million. According to federal law what's 50% AMI (Area Median Income)? For Silicon Valley that's $1.5 million a year. So, if you build a property for one million dollars then sell that house to somebody for a million dollars that's affordable housing? That's an absurd result. And obviously, I'm using the extremes, you know, to a certain extent it never works. It works a little bit, but it's a very blunt instrument. Thankfully it does account for differences like the fact that $1 in Minneapolis doesn't equal a dollar in New York City, you know? That's good that they take that into account, but it's not an effective way to measure affordability, it's just not. What that does for us is get us thinking to assume that that's a ridiculous way to measure affordability. We have to play by those rules to get the public financing, but something else we try to do is look at affordability holistically. Not just in housing, but transportation as well. How much can the folks that live in our housing save in transportation? We try and take it a step further by ensuring that they won't need to have a car to get everywhere. They also won't have to pay the cost of maintaining the car. This is thanks to transit-oriented development. Being able to create housing next to a future light rail station is a good way to do that right? Offer shuttle service to and from the grocery stores… That's going to help out. So, we try to do lots of little things like that to leverage affordability in multiple areas and not just housing. Housing of course is a big one. It's a big cost. And like we said it's a fundamental component of people's lives.

Josh: (In your opinion) what would be an ideal world of housing?

Todd: I think it is one that is filled with a myriad of opportunities...
(The question is), what makes it PLACE? It sounds a little too
abstract to be meaningful, but it's not. There are basic place-making
efforts that make a huge difference as to how space operates. A good
example is people experimenting with putting benches out on the
front yard just to see what happens. Sometimes people are walking
by and think, "let's sit down right there and chat." All of a sudden,
they create these sorts of social squares, you know, and so we put a
lot of thought into the development and meaning of PLACE. It's not
just housing, it's not just stacks of units that people go to. A lot of
thought is put into what sort of place it is. So, for me, a successful
place provides a myriad of opportunities. One example would be
accessibility to finding jobs. We can find a job nearby so you don't
have to commute long distances, spend hours of your life just to get
to this job. Especially if you have a family and you have other
priorities to deal with. Commuting an hour or two one way and back
is hard. So hopefully that includes a job and economic opportunities.
Hopefully that includes the arts and some community because of
that. Hopefully you can look out your window and know that you
have some greenery to look at. And they will have a park nearby
within walking distance to go to and observe some greenery as well.
My sort of personal credo goes to equity and that's what I'm trying to
deliver, and that's what I'm trying to create. It fits well with this
organization.

Martin: To elaborate on your previous point, do you have the same
ideology (in terms of affordable housing) when looking at Greater
Minnesota compared to the Twin Cities?

Todd: Yeah, so it's interesting. There are certainly differences
between the smaller towns and more populous, more dense urban
settings. There's a lot of the small towns in Iowa where housing is
really unaffordable. But how could that be? So, first of all population

by large is moving toward the cities. So those people are moving out of the small towns. Well, that opens up a house that they might have lived in. So, there's some housing available in a lot of these small towns, but nobody's built a new house in 50 years. You may have some houses that are available, and the utilities in these houses are $600 a month. So now, I mean who can afford a six-hundred-dollar utility bill? Not many folks. That's a lot. There are interesting ways in which some of the problems that you see in urban settings actually match rural settings, but maybe for different reasons. But yeah, there is a difference, but by and large I think over the years we've come to an understanding that there are good ways to develop and there are smart ways to develop. One way is density. Density is good. Not everybody wants to live in a dense area, but by and large, the denser an area is, the less money a city spends on infrastructure. For instance, laying one big pipe down to carry water a hundred feet away. And if somebody says, "I want to live in the country, can you please run a pipe, all the way up there?" The city ends up paying for a large share of that. So, density is important, and again multimodal transportation, giving folks options. Not just require them to buy a car, maintain it and drive it 20 miles to go to their job or 20 miles to shop and get food. (In terms of) parking areas, we found that to be very important to people's quality of life. This will apply in a rural setting as well. Obviously with greater density, more people, a lot of times, like, some of the social problems that come, they get magnified just because there's more people, you know, and so that can be really tricky in sort of the larger urban dense spaces, the built environment has been very established (inaudible) become that. So that can be tricky as well, but efforts have been made over the past 20 years to try to develop and use as much of that land as possible. You know, like Kansas City is an interesting city. You look at a picture of Kansas City like 30 or 40 years ago, you see a ridiculous, like half the city is parking lots. Everywhere is just parking lots, and you're like, oh my god. Like, what a terrible use of land right? And now you know real efforts have been made to dig up these parking lots, put some houses in them, some parks, and that's something I recommend you take a look at 60-70 years ago. You can get a sense of how at a macro scale, what their thinking was around like it, it's so auto-oriented, and not people oriented, which is crazy.

Martin: How does housing relate to environmental sustainability in your community?

Todd: We (PLACE board members) are trying to patent this new E-generation process which entails the solar panels and the anaerobic digestion and the greenhouses that go into it. I work with an intellectual property attorney on that. The fundamental idea behind all of that goes to affordability, again, in the holistic sense, so between the solar panels and the energy that is generated from those, and people are also going to eat, and they are going to have food scraps from what they eat, and those are either going to get thrown into a landfill, or they can be thrown into an anaerobic digester that uses the gases and the heat to create energy, so it actually generates energy itself, just like the solar panels do. And all of that energy will go back into the building. So that will lower the utility costs, everybody's electric bills are going to be lower. Through the anaerobic digestion process, there is a by-product that can be used as fertilizer. So that's going to be used in the greenhouses to fertilize the plants there. We would have partners who would come in and do this urban agriculture. So this food that is produced will be turned around and be made available to residents, so they are going to have fresh produce.

So, there is a huge issue that they have discovered over the years: Zoning. Zoning over the years has been like, "this is a commercial area, over here is a residential area, over here we've got houses, over here we've got offices, over here we've got factories…." And historically we want to keep them separate. But what they found over time is that really rigid zoning will make people go to this commercial sector to work, then leave, then you have this whole part of town where nothing is going on during the nights and weekend. So now we are returning to mixed-use stuff, so you have more commercial establishments in the bottom, and houses on top, and 24/7 you have people living, doing stuff, buying stuff, and there is constant activity on, and there's a much better use of the land.

So, what they found over time in part to the zoning issues over the years is that they did not put any thought into people's access to food. You may have heard about food deserts. You think, "how does this apply to our situation in Minnesota? We are in an urban setting but we have a ton of agriculture going around in the metro area. How can there be a food desert?" Well, developments happen, things pop up here and there, and then somebody forgets to build a grocery store, right? So now someone with limited transportation don't have a grocery store nearby to go to, so maybe they are reliant upon the gas station, and there is usually not a lot of great produce at the gas station.   Part of what we're trying to provide with fresh produce is something within walking distance where you will be able to get a head of lettuce right there in your community. Hopefully that will lower foods, hopefully the electrical generation will lower utility costs, and again that all comes down to just trying to save people money and to provide an opportunity for affordable living, not just affordable housing.

Martin: How do you use social justice as a tool to assist in past and current efforts of affordable housing development?

Todd: For me I think it's an organizing principle. It's always been a part of my life. Over the course of your life, there are a lot of different experiences that will touch your heart in a certain way, and maybe help you develop a passion for something. I've been lucky to have multiple, diverse experiences like this too. Between children and adult populations, immigration matters, accessibility issues… I've been very lucky to have been exposed to people from all different walks of life, all different sorts of situations. If you're so fortunate to have that sort of exposure, I think over time we develop this attitude that we're all in this together, but we're all certainly in different places too. We got to be able to help each other out.

Conclusion

Our interview with Todd is more clearly understood when reviewing it along with two theories from our course. First, the Story of Self/Us/Now by Marshall Ganz. We all have a Story of Self. We all have the capacity to learn from each other's stories. The stories that we create usually contain trials and tribulations. We learn to embrace the challenges ahead of us and overcome them. This creates a source of hope and inspiration for the listener. Through various parts of the transcription, we learn that Todd's story of self was impactful for him and the people he chose to work with. The story he encountered when he was interning at the Department of Justice created an everlasting impact on him and his client. His story of self which placed him as an intern at the DOJ and his clients' story of self were an exchange that became a relationship, which is a key principal to community building. Marshall Ganz defines relationships by stating that "relationships can be viewed as exchanges of interests and resources between parties. An exchange becomes a relationship, however, only when a mutual commitment of resources is made to a shared future" (Ganz, 2010, pg. 5).

When a story of self is developed in connection to others, then a story of us is created. According to Marshall Ganz, the questions become, "Why are we called?" and, "What experiences and values do we share as a community that call us to what we are called to?" (Ganz, 2009, p. 16). We see that PLACE's previous efforts have focused on creating a sense of us. Todd shared that they conducted 137 community engagement events for the WAV development in California. Additionally, he followed up by stating they need to ask the same questions they asked the community members in California: "what are you trying to accomplish here?" and, "what input can you provide us that we can use to help you?"

The third piece of Marshall Ganz's theory is the Story of Now. This is considered the action step. Once you have compiled the data you received from your research subjects, this affirms what you thought you knew and more importantly what needs to change. We need to understand the challenge and conflict between the values by which we wish the world lived, and the values by which it actually does. (Ganz, 2009, p. 16)

Ganz believes that once we have woven the fabric of these pieces together, we will be able to work in solidarity towards a common purpose. A purpose that we will be able to achieve one day. Ganz elaborates on the Story of Self by explaining how leadership plays an integral role in the desired outcomes of communities in need:

> Leadership is about enabling others to achieve purpose in the face of uncertainty. When there's certainty, when you know what to do, you don't need leadership. It's when you don't know what to do that the art and creativity of leadership matters. It matters even more in enabling others to work together to achieve a common purpose in the face of uncertainty (Ganz, 2009, p. 18).

As Todd and his fellow board members develop their PLACE neighborhood, they will need to be creative in terms of how to solve the problems that may arise inside the community and outside of it. Todd talked about the strict zoning laws that were enforced and Kansas' flawed urban planning 30 to 40 years ago, which has led to an inability to create mixed-income housing. All of these issues needed to be taken into account when attempting to build community. This brings up the essential question: What are going to be potential roadblocks that PLACE will have to deal with?

Secondly, we have the theory created by Kretzmann and McKnight, the Assets-Based Community Development Model. This theory advances the purpose of building trust amongst neighbors and neighborhood resources for support and strength. Community builders utilize this tool for their assets, hoping to rebuild these local relationships to produce successful community development. Within this community building model, there are two paths that people choose to follow. Both paths are embedded within the transcription.

The first is a common, conventional path. Its primary strategy is "focusing on a community's needs, deficiencies and problems…" (Kretzmann and McKnight, 1996). The illustration painted by Kretzmann and McKnight is the reaction of the average American when they hear the names "South Bronx" and "South Central Los Angeles". The immediately reaction is negative. Some of the images that come to mind are homelessness, welfare dependency, gang-related violence, and abandoned properties. Some of these generalizations are rooted in semi-truths. Kretzmann and McKnight believe they create a "mental map" which enhances the half-truths to the whole truth of that community. Todd addresses the mental map multiple times in the transcript. The first was the hypothetical family who lived next to the Skippy Peanut Butter factory. Once they learned that this dilapidated building was going to be transformed into affordable housing, they subtly winced and felt uncomfortable at the idea. Further, when people would hear about the installation of the imaginary shopping mall in a developing area. People reacted to this in a negative way, saying "the "others" may be shopping or living there, so let's not go there"".

Kretzmann and McKnight explain that the people who create the mental maps are affiliated within public, private and nonprofit human service systems. They deliver a caveat to the reader that these groups are detrimental to the communities they are trying to serve. They create local activities that teach people the inherent nature of their problems, and they believe that they are the ones who will be able to provide the answers. This leads them to believe that their personal and community well-being depend solely upon a client-agency relationship. Kretzmann and McKnight succinctly stated:

> Viewing a community as a nearly endless list of problems and needs leads directly to the much-lamented fragmentation of efforts to provide solutions. It also denies the basic community wisdom which regards problems as tightly intertwined, as symptoms in fact of the breakdown of a community's own problem-solving capacities. (Kretzmann and McKnight, 1996, p. 23).

The second path is encouraged by Kretzmann and McKnight for community builders to follow. It believes in creating "a clear commitment to discovering a community's capacities and assets" (Kretzmann and McKnight, 1996, p. 23). This path shepherds the development of policies and activities based on the capacities, skillsets and assets of marginalized groups and the neighborhoods in which they reside.

Kretzmann and McKnight elaborate, citing historic evidence which shows that community development becomes prevalent when communities are committed to investing in themselves and utilizing their resources in the effort. We can relate to this by referencing the residents of St. Louis Park who approved a home rule charter to make it a city in 1954. As PLACE is fully developed, Todd is hopeful that the mixed-income philosophy partnered with contracted artists will create a sense of solidarity within their community, allowing them to adjust their community when necessary.

The beauty of this step is that community organizers will discover that everyone in the community they are working with has something to offer. They possess an inherent gift. Even though this is something to be recognized, the community organizers need to understand that some of the assets are limited. One of the main examples mentioned was disability. In the interview, Todd showed an innate ability to recognize that those who are differently abled are going to have certain traits that he and every able-bodied person working for PLACE and residing in their complexes need to be cognizant of. They have to understand the limitations that go along with it as well.

Finally, fitting within the second path is the sense of responsibility for the health of the local community, along with mechanisms that allow communities to control certain aspects of the neighborhood. Todd touched on this towards the end of the interview when he discussed community learning, and then applying the tools and principals of environmental sustainability attached to PLACE. Understanding anaerobic digestion, the impact of solar panels, and seeing the positive effects that greenhouses have will all contribute to the communities' social capital and allow them to advocate with neighboring institutions about environmental sustainability.

The PLACE development is currently ready to break ground on their mixed income housing complex. This project has the potential to create community uplift within St. Louis Park. The question is:

How will this project impact the physical and cultural landscape of this city?

About the Author – Martin Beck

I am a social justice enthusiast and recent graduate of the University of St. Thomas in St. Paul, Minnesota. I majored in Justice and Peace Studies and minored in Environmental Sustainability. My academic background aligns with the content contained in this chapter. The experiences I encountered during my undergraduate career fostered my passion to write about PLACE. I interned at a tenant-advocate organization by speaking with constituents about issues ranging from accessible social security disability benefits, securing Section 8 housing, and holding landlords accountable for failing to adhere to basic tenant needs. Following this, I served as an intern in the office of United States Senator, Tina Smith. As a result of my previous work experience, I conducted a mixed-methods study linking recidivism and Minnesota felons. The study focused on the lack of available housing for recently released felons in the metropolitan area and greater Minnesota. In my free time, I like to read, discover new music and continue to learn the intricacies of community organization.

Works Cited:
St. Louis Park (2019). Retrieved from:
      https://www.stlouispark.org/our-city/about-us/history
Ganz, Marshall, 2010, Leading Change: Leadership, Organization, and Social Movements
Ganz, Marshall. (2009). Why stories matter: The art craft of social change. (Organizing for Social Change). Sojourners Magazine, 38(3), 16.
Kretzmann, John, & McKnight, John P., 1996, Assets-Based Community Development. National Civic Review. 85.4 (Winter 1996): p23.
Pinkett, Randal D., & Turner, Nicol E., (2000) Closing the Digital Divide: An Asset- Based Approach to Community Building and Community Technology
United States Census Bureau. "Census of Population and Housing". Archived from the original on April 26, 2015. Retrieved July 23, 2014
      https://www.stlouispark.org/home/showdocument?id=15332.

Who Needs Creative Communities?

  Social justice work has become increasingly more urgent as activists and organizations demand action on the most pressing of issues. Concerns that are getting attention include: housing inequities, access to employment, transportation, and the climate crisis. As conversations surrounding these topics become amplified, organizations within the for-profit and nonprofit sector are called on to fill gaps which community members fall through.

  PLACE is a community developer with 501(c)3 nonprofit status, that is committed to tackling such issues within the community. Their mission statement reads, "... to create places that foster a sustainable, just, and inspiring world" (PLACE). The 501(c)3 designation comes with regulations that state that, "A nonprofit corporation's purpose and activities must serve the organization's mission to benefit the public and may not be operated to profit other persons or entities" (Information). Additionally, nonprofit status shows a commitment to societal betterment beyond monetary gain. With an understanding of the intersectionality of justice issues, PLACE is creating housing options that - in turn - can positively impact various social issues.

  The primary function of PLACE is to offer housing options that can meet the needs of various income levels. Although all income levels are addressed, a higher volume of options lie in more accessible price ranges, "Of our proposed 100 live/work spaces, approximately 60 will be affordable to households below 60% of

AMI (Area Median Income), and 40 of them will be market rate," (PLACE). Local creatives are also members of the community that PLACE is reaching. PLACE has not only committed to creating a physical space that supports creative talent, but also an atmosphere that supports and sees tremendous value in the talents that local creatives possess. PLACE has the capacity to offer housing to individuals of various backgrounds a living space, where meeting people's housing needs can not only be accessible, but also inclusive.

Another role that PLACE recognizes it can step into is related to access to employment. On site jobs can be beneficial to employees, one example being the elimination of transportation costs. In order to create on site jobs, as well as boost the local St. Louis Park economy, PLACE has spaces allotted for a hotel and small other small businesses. Besides job creation, the hotel's purpose is to offer visiting hospital guests a place to stay in the city, at subsidized prices if needed. With various local work options soon to be available, the Met Council formula states estimates that 600 jobs will be created, which includes 119 permanent jobs (PLACE). On site job creation can be a step taken to further break down barriers for community members.

The building plot for PLACE is located with sustainable transportation in mind. The light rail is in the process of creating a light rail extension that will back up to the lot. This will not only promote sustainable transit, but will also give those who live at PLACE access to transit.

In order to further make transit accessible, PLACE is working on creating discounted bus and light rail passes for their residents. The Cedar Lake Bike Trail, a bike path connecting downtown Minneapolis to St. Louis Park also backs up to the site (Cedar). This trail, with the additional possibility of bike sharing, will create another form of sustainable transit for residents. Other transportation options that PLACE hopes to explore includes electric shuttles and car sharing services, with the intention of creating a community that can thrive, car-free. Although, the developer plans to incorporate parking spots for car owning residents, the community is intended to cater to car-free living.

Environmental impacts from infrastructure is one of PLACE's main concerns. Housing can create negative contributions to the environment if not intentionally avoided. In order to combat the negative impacts of infrastructure, PLACE has made it an essential part of the work that they engage in. Green spaces have been proposed in the form of rooftop decks, as well as an urban forest. Green spaces can "... reduce health inequalities, improve well-being, and aid in the treatment of mental illness" (Urban), so their incorporation in an urban community does not go without praise. Additionally, PLACE will be using a form of renewable energy referred to as "E-Generation" (PLACE). The energy generated is created through the use of repurposing food scraps, "which then grows organic produce for distribution via CSA (community supported agriculture)" (PLACE). Lower energy bills coupled with locally grown food, creates various opportunities for local and global positive environmental impact.
PLACE overall shows a commitment to creating inclusive communities by, "provid(ing) the foundation for social, economic, and environmental health that combine together to build community connections, stability, and creativity" (PLACE).

In order to create resources that empower community members of various backgrounds, it is important that organizations like PLACE continue to create sustainable housing options for individuals and families. Organizations need to further recognize the intersection of justice issues, and name this phenomenon, in order to create just solutions.

The United Nations Educational, Scientific, and Cultural Organization (UNESCO) furthers the idea of creative centered, sustainable communities, by their promotion of the "Creative Cities

Network" (UCCN). The UCCN is comprised of 180 cities that have a similar mission of, "placing creativity and cultural industries at the heart of their development plans…" (Creative). UNESCO recognizes that positive societal impact can influence various components in society, when having communities that are focused on the uplifting of various perspectives, with regards to the creative field in which they are involved. Further, there have been positive outcomes that have been associated with creative communities:

- strengthen the creation, production, distribution and dissemination of cultural activities, goods and services;
- develop hubs of creativity and innovation and broaden opportunities for creators and professionals in the cultural sector;
- improve access to and participation in cultural life, in particular for marginalized or vulnerable groups and individuals;
- fully integrate culture and creativity into sustainable development plans. (Creative).

Although there are communities, such as PLACE, that are not "recognized" by UNNC, there is still space for organizations to create, creatively minded communities.

These communities have been recognized for their inclusivity, shared learning spaces, and community support, which are all values that can transcend a business designation or award. Overall, creative communities have the capacity to make, "…balanced development in economic, cultural, environmental and social terms". (Creative), but cities need organizations to recognize the importance of such betterment and be willing to invest in empowering and justice-oriented community building.

About the Author - Mackenna Cristilly

I am currently studying Justice and Peace Studies and General Business at the University of St. Thomas. I have a passion for community building and sustainable, justice oriented, business models. In the future, I hope to pursue a master's program that can further enforce these passions.

Works Cited

Cedar Lake LRT Regional Trail. (n.d.). Retrieved December 18, 2019, from https://www.threeriversparks.org/location/cedar-lake-lrt-regional-trail.

Creative Cities: Creative Cities Network. (n.d.). Retrieved December 18, 2019, from https://en.unesco.org/creative-cities/.

Information for Nonprofits. (n.d.). Retrieved December 18, 2019, from https://www.ag.state.mn.us/Charity/InfoNonProfits.asp.

PLACE. (n.d.). Retrieved December 18, 2019, from https://www.welcometoplace.org/.

Urban green spaces. (2016, August 4). Retrieved December 18, 2019, from https://www.who.int/sustainable-development/cities/health-risks/urban-green-space/en/.

People of PLACE

In order to build housing that actually benefits our communities, and specifically benefits the people that haven't had access to wealth, we need to realize that housing has been used as a tool by the largely privileged classes, to actually concentrate wealth in their communities and perpetuate it.
- Abby Alldaffer

When Abby was only 5 years old, her family purchased a 1970s split-level home in what she ironically refers to as the "poor area" of Maple Grove, a suburb located just 30 minutes Northwest of the Twin Cities. The prefabricated home with a pool and forest for a backyard was enormous compared to the apartments they had previously rented. She recounts the experience as "a weird dissonance" when considering the median household income in Maple Grove was around $70,000 and most families rented or owned single-family homes when she lived there.

During my interview with Abby, she shared stories regarding her childhood home, which her parents still occupy today. She described the joy of playing with friends in her backyard and even said they once built a Bridge to Terabithia. Similar to popular children's story, Abby and her friends used the imaginary world of Terabithia to escape the woes of everyday life.

The physical structure of my house was pretty stable. But the familial life inside was not necessarily as stable.

At the time, the split-level home largely represented her family dynamic. Abby's mother spent most of her time upstairs while her father spent most of his time in the basement. This left little room for Abby and her younger sister to call their own.

I felt ownership over my house, but I didn't really feel ownership over the space.

When Abby was 14 years old, her father introduced her to SketchUp, a 3D modeling software program. She made models of houses regularly using SketchUp and even told her family that she wanted to be a real estate agent. That was when they recommended architecture.

Architecture initially was just me imagining a house that was safe and felt like home.

Years later, Abby went on to study architecture at the University of Minnesota. It was here that she learned the reality of the architectural industry – it is profit driven and generally doesn't prioritize justice and equity, values Abby personally adopted after recognizing her own privileges regarding housing. While in college, Abby began looking for opportunities where she could combine creativity and architecture with her newfound commitment to justice. It was at this point that she found PLACE. Their model, which is driven by equity, sustainability, access, and justice, aligns perfectly with her values.

During our interview, Abby shared that her ancestors owned land and slaves, and that as a result, she has access to generational wealth, a privilege she grapples with regularly in her work with PLACE. She suggests that "Ownership of housing has been a representation of wealth in society," and that ownership itself is an inequitable system.

In order for us to build housing that's accessible ... we need to recognize that where it comes from isn't entirely just. And, especially in America, not just at all to minority populations.

Abby believes that if you've experienced injustice, you're more likely to recognize housing injustice as the product of a broken system and not the fault of an individual. Although she believes that people need to have initiative, Abby also argues that we need to "make it easier for people to engage with a system that's not built for them." Something she gets to do regularly with PLACE.

We're building for everybody regardless of income, regardless of race, regardless of gender.

During one of her first shifts as a volunteer with PLACE, she attended a community meeting with a group of single mothers transitioning out of homelessness. Seeing how her colleagues explained what PLACE does in such a sensitive and empathetic way made her want to get involved even more. In 2017, PLACE hired Abby for an entry level position with a salary of $24,000. The modest pay gave her the chance to experience housing with similar means as the people they plan to serve. Given that PLACE is a non-hierarchical organization and does not employ titles other than "executive team member," Abby has been able to gain skills in other areas of development. She credits both PLACE and her exploratory streak for allowing her to enter communities and see them for what they are instead of projecting her own ideas of what they should look like and how they should function.

In Abby's words, housing is "not just about the house. It's also about how we provide the services to the people inside the house." For Abby, her work with PLACE is tied directly to her own housing experience.

*I want to create homes for people where they feel
comfortable and safe ... and for a large part of my life I
didn't necessarily have that.*

She believes that a portion of the people PLACE plans to serve will
have felt similar to how she did in her childhood home.

*They have some semblance of a home, but what's really
missing is that stability and that connection to the place.*

A connection PLACE is attempting to establish.

When asked what housing initiatives need in terms of
leadership, Abby said, "There needs to be more collaboration,
interorganizationally [sic]." She emphasizes the need "to work at a
local level to come together to access resources that might not be
available if we were just an individual or one organization." A large
portion of the resources she is referring to are financial.

*Housing in general is not viewed as a human right by society
and by our economy, it's more viewed as a commodity that
people can buy into.*

Additionally, Abby believes it's important for housing initiatives to
have direct experience with the communities they serve and that the
plans they create should respect the community and build to what
they need – a fundamental practice of PLACE.

What works for one person doesn't work for another person.

This practice is known as assets-based community development.

Assets-Based Community Development

Massive economic shifts have resulted in the movement of industrial jobs away from central cities and their neighborhoods. In their article titled "Assets-based community development," Kretzmann and McKnight, claim these jobs are being replaced with both highly professionalized jobs that require elaborate education and credentials for entry, and "routine, low-paying service jobs without much of a future" (Kretzmann & McKnight, 1996). As a result, low-income neighborhoods are being forced to rebuild their communities to create new opportunities for socioeconomic growth.

The traditional path to community development, and that most taken, focuses on identifying a community's needs, deficiencies and problems. The challenge with this path is that it requires substantial financial and human resources and does not address the root of the problem. This approach to community development relies on external entities to identify the needs of the neighborhood, teach the community about those needs, and offer services to meet them. According to Kretzmann and McKnight, this approach is problematic because "residents come to believe that their well-being depends upon being a client" and they no longer feel they have the agency to take control of their own community (Kretzmann & McKnight, 1996). Additionally, they argue that "Viewing a community as a nearly endless list of problems and needs leads directly to the much lamented fragmentation of efforts to provide solutions" (Kretzmann & McKnight, 1996). At best, this needs-based strategy only guarantees survival and rarely leads to serious change or community development.

The alternative, which Abby alluded to in her interview, is known as assets-based community development. This approach focuses on developing policies and activities based on the capacities, skills, and assets of communities. Instead of depending on outside resources to create solutions, assets-based community development puts the power in the hands of the community. According to

Kretzmann and McKnight, "significant community development takes place only when local community people are committed to investing themselves and their resources in the effort" (Kretzmann & McKnight, 1996). In communities that recognize and mobilize their assets, community members will function, not as clients, but as full contributors to the community-building process. Only when we replace the traditional deficient-oriented approach will we begin to see communities flourish in opportunity and the possibility of advancement.

About the Author – Amaris Holguin

I am a first-generation college student at the University of St. Thomas pursuing degrees in communication and journalism and justice and peace studies. These areas of study reflect my passion for social justice and allow me to continue analyzing the dynamics of inequity in our society. After college, I hope to further my education by pursuing a master's degree in Human Rights or Public Policy.

Works Cited

A. Alldaffer, personal communication, October 18, 2019.

Kretzmann, J., & McKnight, J. P. (1996). Assets-based community development. National Civic Review, 85(4), 23+. Retrieved from https://link-gale-com.ezproxy.stthomas.edu/apps/doc/A19212826/EAIM?u=clic_stthomas&sid=EAIM&xid=8fb82653

Beyond Faces and Places

HOME IS WHERE THERE IS ONE TO LOVE US

Home's not merely four square walls,
Though with pictures hung and gilded;
Home is where Affection calls—
Filled with shrines the Hearth hath builded!
Home! Go watch the faithful dove,
Sailing 'neath the heaven above us.
Home is where there's one to love!
Home is where there's one to love us.

Home's not merely roof and room,
It needs something to endear it;
Home is where the heart can bloom,
Where there's some kind of lip to cheer it!
What is home with none to meet,
None to welcome, none to greet us?
Home is sweet, and only sweet,
Where there's one we love to meet us!

- Charles Swain

How does your identity shape your experience of community? At first, this question may seem all-too broad, and maybe slightly immobilizing. "Single, white, straight female. What does that mean for my community? Uh, I don't know" (C. Rice, personal communication, November 7, 2019). But with some space to think and wrestle with what identity and community truly mean, we may come to look differently at how we are intricately connected to the world and people around us.

For Carley Rice, her identity and community once came from where she lived. Growing up in a small town in Michigan, some of her best friends lived in the same little subdivision, and pretty much all of her family lived within a 25-mile radius, max. Her sense of community was so incredibly tied to location for most of her life, but that is not the case anymore. After completing a Bachelors Degree in biology and environmental studies, and then a masters in sustainability, she made the move from rural Michigan to urban Minnesota based off of a recommendation from a life-long friend. Since moving to the Twin Cities, she's found that "it's kind of interesting that, to me, my neighborhood is just where I live. And that's it" (C. Rice, personal communication, November 7, 2019). Due to the similar culture throughout the Midwest, this distinction likely does not draw from differences between Michigan and Minnesota, but from rural and urban. Rice says that "when you live in a small town, you really have no choice but to know the people that are around you. When you're in a big city, it's like I'm living in a building with maybe 100 other people, and I don't know a single one of their names" (C. Rice, personal communication, November 7, 2019). Instead, her community now largely stems from her workplace at Spark-Y, a Twin Cities-based nonprofit that empowers youth through hands-on education rooted in sustainability and entrepreneurship. She deeply enjoys being surrounded by individuals who have such similar interests and passions but can also relate to familiar struggles and hardships.

—

After growing up within a community linked by location, it is no-doubt something to be missed and desired in this space and season of life too. Rice reminisced of how she misses "being able to, you know, walk down the street and know who owns the bar, the coffee shop. Yeah, and know the people that are driving past you. There's something about that that's very comforting" (C. Rice, personal communication, November 7, 2019). When living in a city, is it really necessary to forgo this sense of community altogether? When you're in a small space filled with so many people, what barriers are making community-building so much harder in a city setting?

In considering where this sense of place got lost in translation in the move from rural to urban, we discussed what an ideal housing situation might look like here in Minneapolis. Before jumping into the depths of possibilities of what housing can provide to individuals and communities, Rice articulated how structures in our society favor some over others, and that ideal living situations may look different for everyone. Our life experiences shape how we look at issues or advantages related to housing. She has experienced first-hand some of the problems faced in the housing market in the Twin Cities. The first and most immediate frustration concerns cost of living. She voiced how "the fact that what I'm paying in rent, I could get a three-bedroom house where I'm from, is a rude awakening" (C. Rice, personal communication, November 7, 2019). Although she recognized her own privilege in having the ability to have an apartment in the city, she understood this housing struggle that many face. The lack of availability of fresh food is a very real and imminent issue as well. From personal experience, Rice notes that "There's one grocery store that's technically in walkable distance. You know, walkable for me, but not walkable for maybe an old lady down the street" (C. Rice, personal communication, November 7, 2019). Outside of the realm of personal experience, Rice's passion for the environment and sustainability give her a unique outlook on how these topics are closely intertwined with housing as well. She acknowledged that "environmental justice is very real in the Twin Cities. But as far as personal experience, I've been on the greener side of history, just based on who I am and what I look like. Which is not fair" (C. Rice, personal communication, November 7, 2019).

In the midst of all these struggles, we can find hope through our capacity to enact change. Without hesitation, the ideal housing situation for Rice would be "what PLACE is trying to do in St. Louis Park" (C. Rice, personal communication, November 7, 2019). Some qualities that she mentioned include: a neighborhood with green space, easy access to public transportation, walkable to an affordable grocery store, accessibility, sustainable practices wherever possible, and removing class barriers by integrating people of different income levels. Above all, affordability is the greatest concern. And "not having to live in 250 square feet to have it be affordable" (C. Rice, personal communication, November 7, 2019). Don't we all deserve a place to live; a house to make a home?

Many apartment buildings are devoid of a lobby, much less a community space to study, play, work, interact, or live in. Land and space are seen as precious commodities, especially in the city, but dedicating more of it to communal spaces could provide a great deal of shared benefit as well. The intangibility of community makes it an asset often overlooked in planning processes. Open spaces, whether they be physical or relational, devoted to the sharing of ideas and experiences hold power. They hold power to increase wellbeing and productivity, improve work and personal lives, and to give people the permission to be creative. Open space provides the opportunity to create new relationships and do life together. Not everyone has a consistent home-base for an extended time, but that could be an asset to creating community, rather than just a barrier. New faces don't have to remain new if we have and seize the opportunity to be intentional in whatever space and time we find ourselves in. Home is not just the walls that house our possessions, but the people and places that hold pieces of our hearts. Those walls and rooms mean exponentially more when there's one we love to meet us there.

Carly Rice

In his book entitled "The Moral Imagination," John Paul Lederach examines the concept of the moral imagination and describes it as "something rooted in the challenges of the world yet capable of giving birth to that which does not yet exist" (Lederach, 2005, p. 29). This process involves four main components: imagining ourselves in a web of relationships, the potential to maintain a paradoxical curiosity, providing space to pursue creativity, and an acceptance of the risk involved in stepping into unfamiliar spaces (Lederach, 2005, p. 5). Although this theory is presented in the context of overcoming systems of violence and pursuing a more just future, it is also particularly applicable in relation to community building and turning a new city, neighborhood, or house into a home.

The first idea that Lederach presents involves the centrality of relationships. Often times when cycles of violence are broken, it is imperative for individuals and communities involved to develop the capacity to imagine themselves as a part of a web of relationships, involving anyone from their own families to their greatest enemies. We must recognize that "ultimately the quality of life is dependent on the quality of life of others" (Lederach, 2005, p. 35). The well-being of ourselves, our children, grandchildren, and loved ones in any respect is directly tied to that of our neighbors, our co-workers, even our adversaries. When we wrestle with how to develop connections to those around us, we should first recognize how we are already connected to them. Even with, and perhaps because of, our differences, our lives matter to each other, no matter how obvious or deeply those connections lie.

In order to understand the meaning of paradoxical curiosity, it's helpful to first examine what these words mean separately. A paradox "suggests that truth lies in but also beyond what is initially perceived" (Lederach, 2005, p. 36). It brings together supposedly unrelated ideas in a way that prompts the uncovering of some greater truth. Cultivating curiosity elicits a desire to look more deeply and thoughtfully at how we see the world — whether we believe we already understand something fully or not. When these terms are brought together, paradoxical curiosity "approaches social realities with an abiding respect for complexity, a refusal to fall prey to the pressures of forced dualistic categories of truth, and inquisitiveness about what may hold together seemingly contradictory social energies in a greater whole" (Lederach, 2005, p. 36). This can be used to question circumstances such as living in a building with hundreds of others and not knowing any of them personally. While it is necessary to take the current situation at face value, it is also essential to continue forward on a path towards understanding on a heart-level of how these circumstances came to be, and how we individually and collectively can, should, and will progress.

Along with recognizing the centrality of relationships and pursuing a sense of paradoxical curiosity, we must work to provide space for creativity. Encouraging imagination pushes us to envision new "avenues of inquiry and ideas about change that require us to think about how we know the world, how we are in the world, and most important, what in the world is possible" (Lederach, 2005, p. 39). This also involves a willingness to risk, to embrace the unknown and what all that may bring. Creating space can come about in a variety of ways. It may be interpersonal, mental, or physical. In the context of housing, this could look like the affordability and presence of communal living spaces. It may be a culture of interest, communication, and collective pursuit of understanding. Individually, we may need to allow ourselves to take a step back from the mundane routines we find ourselves stuck in and allow ourselves to see and utilize the value in being intentional with our thoughts, time, and relationships. It is clear that this can be uncomfortable, as noted by Lederach. We have to risk our own comfort found in the known and familiar in order to grow and seek something greater, not only for ourselves, but for the webs of relationships that we establish and construct on a daily basis.

The moral imagination provides a framework as to how individuals and communities can seek change and contribute to a more meaningful and just future. This structure can be used not only to dismantle systems of injustice, but as a tool to bring to life the meaningful connections and common understanding that we all long for. It might just allow us to turn neighbors into friends, people that feel like family, and cultivate a sense of "home" to return to — no matter where you are.

About the Author - Jackie Resh

I am a student at the University of Saint Thomas, pursuing a double major in Justice & Peace Studies and Business, with a minor in Sustainability. My passions for people, social justice, and working towards solutions for a more equitable world shape who I am today and how I want to contribute to society in the future.

Works Cited

Lederach, J. P. (2010). The moral imagination: the art and soul of building peace. Oxford: Oxford University Press.
Swain, C. (1937). Home Is Where There Is One to Love Us. In H. Felleman (Ed.), The Best Loved Poems of the American People (pp. 380). Doubleday.

Leadership in Housing Policy

Social justice depicts fairness as it manifests in society. Fairness ranges throughout all aspects that make life comfortable in society, from housing, healthcare, race, gender and employment among others. Social justice aims at protecting and respecting every person's rights and affording them equal opportunities in the society. Elizabeth Bowling has been able to make use of her skills in advocacy and public policy to help co-found PLACE a nonprofit organization that seeks to team up and join forces with most cities to develop diverse income, transit focused developments on affordable living opportunities for most low income wage earners as well as feature arts in the developments (PLACE, 2019 accessed at welcometoplace.org). Her contribution on social justice has been immense in the United States, and her push to have everyone around her take part in the development of the Country, is a positive use of her abilities to mobilize resources to help in achieving social justice in the housing sector.

Her commitment to social justice in the housing, coupled with her vast experience in promoting equity, policy development and resource mobilization helped transform the vocational support services that aimed at extending the reach to many people who were homeless and suffering. Her impact was hugely critical and very essential for the Minnesota Department of Rehabilitation Services. Considering that housing globally has not become a reality, and it is still an important social justice issue in the contemporary times,

Elizabeth Bowling helps to bridge the inequality in access to housing. These inequalities have held back many low-income earners in the society limiting their access to other social amenities such access to quality health care and education. These unequal opportunities often give rise to social injustice. She takes personal responsibility individually and collectively with other members' in her organization to share a purpose of achieving affordable housing in the face of uncertainty.

Elizabeth says that, "social justice is the principle that all persons, irrespective of their inherent characteristics or their means, are to be treated equitably, with integrity, and without prejudice, transforming justice extended to the individual into justice for all. I think of it as best practice for optimizing human potential." Elizabeth Bowling co-founded PLACE as a means to create interpersonal relationships that linked her to other individuals, networks and organizations that created a fabric that helped push and reform the housing policies. This was necessary to ensure every citizen gained access to shelter, since it is a basic need. Elizabeth Bowling invested her time and her skills in policy development and advocacy to help further the idea of affordable housing to the low-income earners as that is the only means to achieve social justice in society. Her experience of helping the homeless in the Minnesota Department of Rehabilitation Services impacted to her positively in her commitment and push for better housing projects in low income areas alongside with other projects that provided employment to the residents living in the low-cost housing areas.

However, she could not affect all the change she needed in housing and that posed a serious challenge towards her pursuit of a goal she so held dear to her life. She felt that lack of decent and affordable housing was a collective responsibility and not just an effort of those who could not afford it. She cut out her identity and made a choice to help secure social justice by ensuring equitable and affordable access top decent housing. This demanded that various approaches need to be incorporated if all the people from the various backgrounds and social had to be incorporated to push for a single goal and process that would result in sustainability, equity, affordability and accessibility to housing by all members of the society.

Her voice in the housing debate did not only tell of her part in helping towards the shared vision of affordable housing but helped many other key players in the housing industry to lend a voice and collectively help remove the pains of the members of society who could not afford decent housing as a result of their income status. This is a major reflection on the pain suffered by our society and the inability to ensure equity across all our people (Ganz, 2010).

After realizing many people shared a similar goal like herself, she set on to cofound PLACE to help bring people with overlapping stories together and achieve the common goal they had of affordable and decent housing. Her organization had diverse players from diverse backgrounds under her able leadership that expressed similar values and experiences and shared the collective identity. The common challenges they faced and the experiences of injustice in society inspired the organization to make their contribution and be part of the larger American vision of ensuring decent and affordable housing to every citizen within the corners of the country.

Housing is a common factor that affects all the other aspects of life such as health care, which is very critical in the livelihoods of citizens. The larger American goal is to ensure that every citizen of their society has access to decent housing. Accessibility to housing was therefore a very essential step towards ensuring social justice in the society. This is also largely because; housing contributes significantly to the creation of jobs, opening up of new tax revenues for the society besides increasing the local purchasing power. This therefore offers an equal opportunity for the homeless and the low income earners in our community to save their money, gain access to the essential affordable housing units and get the opportunity to access jobs such as the hotel industry that come as a result of the housing units. Effecting that change needed an interpreter of the shared experience in Elizabeth Bowling, who continues to offer a critical leadership role ranging from the choices the organizations makes, which is built from the founding goal, through their challenges and the results the organization continues to achieve (Leonard & McLaren, 2002).

The common challenge to all the members in the organization was the urgency to implement the values they shared together at PLACE. They had to make a commitment to design and construct both low income and high-income development that features both affordable living opportunities and arts. Their commitment as an organization was to ensure every community member participates and contributes to their own empowerment in every aspect of development that was undertaken by PLACE. Their commitment in financing and building housing units for the general public is as a result of their collective will to create places that ensures a sustainable, just and inspiring society.

However, the risk that is associated with the urgency of developing the mixed income housing units sometimes is political. They can be as a result of laws and policies that control development, edging out areas that predominantly inhabited by the low-income earners. However, continued efforts in policy shaping are bearing fruits and spaces are given to individuals and organizations to impact on the housing industry. This comes with a hope to the many citizens who have suffered social injustice for far too long. The hope is that today St. Louis Park, in the Twin Cities is experiencing tremendous changes. Hundreds of both low- and high-income apartments are being constructed by PLACE in a bid to provide affordable living and working housing units for art, luxury units and permanent supportive housing units for the low-income families within the region (Deborah Besser, P.E). This is besides a hotel that will ensure that the needs of travelers who require easy access to other regions with low prices are catered, besides providing employment to the residents of the area to work in the hotel. They also provide E-generation technology that supports the entire community with renewable energy drastically lowering their bills on utilities. The project is also built in a strategic position to where a probable light rail will be constructed and the car free options availability.

The urgency in the social injustice in housing is also a matter of Interest I took in since I share the identity with those pushing for affordable housing units such as the PLACE organization. My interaction with an expert in the housing development sector and a champion on social justice is beneficial in examining stories and the approaches that have for long remained unexamined or faced bias in their discussion. This is also very critical in promoting voice, planning and decision making. Contributions from the various players besides PLACE and the community members is very fundamental in helping problematize underlying aspects that may create bias and develop assumptions that may result in social injustice. This biasness has been existent especially at the policy level, which ultimately affects how development is done at community levels. Comparing the different stories from the various actors provide different world views and help the intersectional identities identify what frustrates collaboration and prevents reconciliation in terms of approaches (Klein, 2018). This has given PLACE a different view on collaboration. The results of collaboration were seen when they developed the mixed income creative community in Ventura together with members of the community living there. Collaboration with the final consumers of any development ensures sustainability as members of the community would own the project.

The project was a series of more than 100 public meetings with the members of the society, especially the local community living there which resulted in the landmark project that provides affordable working and living units for many members in the creative arts and their families, getting out of homelessness. The neighborhood speaks of a hopeful venture since it attracts tourists and has become a vibrant economy where majority of the residents are getting jobs. Besides that, the voices from the many views of the actors help in identifying gaps that may have been left out by particular groups and unravel the power dynamics that often results in oppression. Voices also help us recognize the realities when it comes to inequality in access to housing and other aspects of humanity such as environmental degradation and oppression, a critical aspect that is useful in planning and pushing for reforms in housing especially in other regions the project may not have impacted.

Dynamic leadership calls for leaders to take ownership of their sphere of influence to cause change in society. This happens when a leader uses the abilities they possess to empower the lives of others. Elizabeth Bowling and the PLACE community play a very fundamental role in community building, helping to cultivate relationships and encourage shared experiences that ensure common commitment to a shared vision. Her skills are very useful and necessary for both the organization and her community. She uses her professional abilities to focus on improving housing as a tool to achieve social justice in society. As a co-founder of PLACE, she continues to transform the livelihoods of the people in the community by ensuring stable and affordable housing and affording a chance for the low-income earners to have a creative and inclusive community to live in. Elizabeth plays a critical role in ensuring change in policy, getting involved in research activities as well as building the affordable houses for the homeless and providing employment opportunities within the communities where the houses are built. Her capacity as a positional leader for PLACE and a co-founder makes it easier for her to make critical decisions and contributions towards housing in the country. Her push and commitment are informed by her desire and experiences she went through while working in the Minnesota Department of Rehabilitation Services.

Most of the housing projects are informed by the painful history of members of the community have suffered from inequality and inability to have access to affordable housing units that greatly affected their other aspects of life such as education, access to health care and generally their health (Mueller et al., 2007). The history of housing is therefore essential to Elizabeth since it helps her in seeking to understand and expose the systems that continue to perpetuate injustice as well as finding out the causal factors that are responsible for lack of housing and other social injustices. These are mostly actions of how power plays out in systems which are political. Inequalities resulting from power dynamics affect the economy greatly.

Economics play a major role in ensuring housing as a basic need for the members of any society. The growth of an economy and increase in the income of the citizens of any country means that those people are able to allocate most of their funds towards getting a decent house. It also pushes demand for housing upwards (Shlay,1995). However, when the economy is doing badly, many people will not have the money to spend on getting a decent house and would instead focus on other primary needs which are essential in supporting life. This means that decisions on economics affect many players who want to contribute towards social justice and equity in the society, since it is a governance and political decision. Housing therefore is equally a political issue since it is policy and resource allocation that determines whether they get built or not. And since politics is participatory, it therefore means that the first step to governance must begin with voting. This is critical in decision making where many citizens can contribute to decision making (Klein, 2015). Public transport systems considerably affect the cost of housing and most often makes it more expensive to afford houses within the reach of public transit areas. However, public transport may also spur the development of housing units as most people would want to live within public amenities such as cheaper transit lines. Elizabeth plays a critical role both as a person and her organization in shaping the policies related to housing and in doing the actual construction of housing units and other social economic infrastructure that offers employment to the low-income earners in the society.

Elizabeth Bowling finds Individual identities to be very essential because it helps her intentionally take steps that are useful for her in understanding social injustice from various perspectives. She is able to understand and recognize that oppression, inequality, poverty religion among other elements require an honest understanding and assessment of our value systems and faith systems in society that contribute to nurturing an unjust system. Individual identities will help us unravel those unjust political, social and economic systems and their structures are as a result of ineffective value systems that need to be changed. PLACE therefore continues to be an effective identity in exposing the imbalance and inequalities in our economic system because of the unjust allocation of resources, the imbalance in the political system by limiting engagement with majority community members thus elbowing out their participation in their own democratic governance and lastly the inequalities and imbalance due to our social status by limiting access to affordable housing units for the low income earners members of our community.

Elizabeth Bowling has been able to build on her profile and that has helped her develop reasons why other regions are underdeveloped. Her theory is based on her understanding of the political, social and economic sectors of our country and how they are woven together to carefully ensures that inequality and imbalances is the end product of the processes. This web of complex interlocking privileges and oppressions have the long-term effects of creating a very unstable society that is coupled with poverty, inequality and injustice.

Exposing the underlying aspects that necessitate oppression and injustice helps in the analysis of values that never get examined and have to problematize biases that change the emergent patterns. This critical evaluation of underlying issues of bias will help in understanding why certain policies in housing are undertaken and why such discrepancies affect housing.

The danger of a single story helps us also to wholly understand the factors that necessitate the inequalities that surround affordable housing. It helps point out that an individual understands that the policy makers and those responsible in the distribution of resources may not give the exact picture of the reasons of such imbalances. Finding a common ground may give a clear understanding of the causal factors and that will help in resolving the housing debacle. Housing in sustainable communities requires the people have access to affordable housing and working units while they are also able to get employment within the same community. An example is the development of housing units where local artists can get access and develop their arts will attract tourists and grow the economy, assuring the members of the community of employment. She describes that a single perspective makes that the definitive perspective of the story (Adichie, 2009).

The contribution of the concept of Adichie in the danger of a single story is critical in understanding the imbalance in housing. From the perspective of her concept, it will unfair to conclude that the imbalance in housing is a result of inequality in distribution of resources. Housing may not only be affected by the distribution of resources but also by the availability of the same resources. It is impossible to distribute resources that are not themselves available.

Creating the two contrasting perspectives is of great significance in explaining the reasons for the inadequacies in affordable houses. The suggestion that Political systems are responsible for the inadequacy in housing may also prove incomplete according to Adichie's the danger of a single story. Political systems may be willing to pursue the agenda of constructing mixed income housing across many regions but other priority areas such as health, which cannot be ignored takes the priority.

Changes in policy will lead to a balance in access to affordable housing. Ideally policies are the most essential tools to implement changes needed in society. However, the concept disagrees, that changes alone may not affect the changes most people require in the society. A collaborative approach by the various stakeholders with similar identities will help pursue and implement the changes that are needed in society to develop affordable and sustainable housing and working units for both high- and low-income earners in the society.

Individual and intersectional identities are catalysts for reform that will inform development in housing. Focusing on the contribution from individuals and organizations and movements may not in themselves the catalysts for change. This is because, some identity organizations work with volunteers. Making them become accountable to their commitments may prove futile. This can therefore derail the collective push for reforms in housing. Besides, reforms are also affected when the economy is doing well. Pushing for reforms at a time the economy is wanting may not necessitate the outcome required. To quote Elizabeth Bowling, she alludes that "social justice is the principle that all persons, irrespective of their inherent characteristics or their means, are to be treated equitably, with integrity, and without prejudice, transforming justice extended to the individual into justice for all. I think of it as best practice for optimizing human potential."

This concept is therefore very essential in explaining the expectations required from everyone in development of sustainable housing in the community.

Personal understanding may be rooted and may have an effect of colonialism, misogyny, agorophobia and others. Making use of tools such as gender, human rights and critical theory will make us examine our normative commitments and the normative worldview of others to unravel the deeply anchored bias, look at ways to work together and help in achieving common goals such as social justice and thus promoting social justice elements such as housing. Housing is a critical element of social justice. It is therefore essential that everybody should have access to affordable housing if social justice has to be achieved.

The ethical issues that arise from housing involve ensuring affordable housing units for low income earners and ensuring equity across all the categories of individuals within a society if social justice has to be achieved. Decisions on scarce allocation of resources ought to be made in consideration of beneficence, autonomy and justice to all the members of the society (Iglasias, 2007). However, developments in the economic and the political structure in the United States have impacted heavily in the housing system. Complaints and concerns on the conditions of the housing system are decisions made by the political class on their day to day democracy in the administration of the country. The complexities that come with ethical allocation of resources on housing, directly impacts on the ability to afford every citizen a decent housing unit. Decent housing units should have accessibility to affordable transit systems that will ease their pressure on money while making their mobility quite cheap ensuring social justice. It is therefore only moral that allocation of resources must follow a process that includes distributive justice, especially from policy makers and those in management of resources.

Giving voice to values is an important approach in persuading the people involved in policy shaping, making and those who exercise the daily democracy in distribution of resources meant to be of public benefit. Adding my voice will positively influence my subject to capture the aspects of my story that they may have not thought about and will help develop a better script on the neglected areas that needs attention. My voice will also greatly influence the development of ethical action plans meant to leverage the economic imbalance that will ensure that social injustice in the housing sector is achieved and that every citizen gets an opportunity to access a decent housing unit at an affordable price. My voice will equally contribute towards development of skills useful in pushing for the common goal of ensuring equity and a balanced society in terms of development.

However, sometimes the lack of my understanding on the complexities involved in allocation of resources may invoke me to lend a voice that may negatively impact and derail the contribution of other players in pushing for affordable housing to many regions within the United States. If my contribution fails to capture integral issues affecting not only housing but also aspects such as the level of income and accessibility to affordable transit systems such as rail lines, it may still prove to be a burden on the shoulders of the low income earners who may find it expensive to live in the housing units provided. It therefore demands that while making a contribution on the aspect of housing, a special attention must also be given to other areas that are directly linked with housing. Providing a voice on the reforms and the steps needed in ensuring affordable houses are provided without the necessary experience and knowledge on the complexity of housing may deal a major blow in the development of housing. This is because, I may likely leave out critical aspects of planning which is very essential in determining where and how to construct the mixed income housing and whether the community around will have a transit system that connects them to other regions easily and affordably.

My perspective in the issue of housing is very critical in adding a voice and creating a collective identity with other people that is useful in pushing for changes in policies and allocation of resources that will help in the development of mixed income housing and a connected transit system on it. However, if my voice is not connected to the voices of other individuals pushing for reforms, I may derail the whole process of lending a voice towards a common goal.

A commitment to shape the vision of a large organization of volunteers and staff joined by a common vision demands that every member becomes accountable to the commitment they make towards furthering the common goal of the organization. Elizabeth Bowling's contribution and commitment in the PLACE organization paints the picture of an accomplished leader with the right strategy and character to pursue what she aims for a and also to lead other towards achieving the common goal of ensuring sustainability, equity and access to affordable housing units.

About the Author – Jack Joa

I am a Student at The University of Saint Thomas, studying Political Science and Justice & Peace Studies. My focus is around the use of public policy to help address social injustices.

Works Cited:

Adichie, C. N. (2009). The danger of a single story.

Besser, D., & Welt, T., & Dasyam, H., & Shealy, T. (2019, June), Sustainability Service Learning as a Mechanism for Acquiring New Knowledge Paper presented at 2019 ASEE Annual Conference & Exposition , Tampa, Florida. https://peer.asee.org/33330

Ganz, M. (2010). Leading change: Leadership, organization, and social movements. Handbook of leadership theory and practice, 19, 1-10.

Iglesias, T. (2007). Our pluralist housing ethics and the struggle for affordability. Wake Forest L. Rev., 42, 511.

Klein, M. (Ed.). (2015). Democratizing Leadership: Counterhegemonic Democracy in Communities, Organizations and Institutions. IAP.

Klein, M., Finnegan, A., & Nelson-Pallmeyer, J. (2018). Circle of Praxis Pedagogy for Peace Studies. Peace Review, 30(3), 270-278.

Leonard, P., & McLaren, P. (Eds.). (2002). Paulo Freire: A critical encounter. Routledge.

Mueller, E. J., & Tighe, J. R. (2007). Making the case for affordable housing: Connecting housing with health and education outcomes. Journal of Planning Literature, 21(4), 371-385. PLACE, 2019 accessed at welcometoplace.org

Looking Past the Prickly

Sarah Nelson, 2019

The Purple Sea Urchin is a small, dark, prickly and poisonous creature that lives at the bottom of the sea among kelp forests off of the coasts of the Pacific Ocean. When asked about important animals in ecosystems, it would be rare for anyone to mention these odd creatures. As humans, we typically equate poisonous with bad or scary, but these tiny creatures are vital to their ecosystems. Purple Sea Urchins graze on kelp litter, allowing the kelp forests stay healthy so they can grow and thrive. These kelp forests are home to a myriad of fish and shellfish species all of which ensure ocean health. The urchins also are the main food source for the sea otter, the keystone species in their ecosystems

(Pearse, 2006). Without looking at the bigger picture, one may mistake Purple Sea Urchins as not only insignificant, but even harmful due to their prickly nature. However, knowing the bigger picture helps us to understand they are an integral part of a healthy ecosystem. As Purple Sea Urchins are important to their ecosystem, so are the sometime prickly voices of opposition and concern to PLACE's leadership role in the community of St. Louis Park.

The voice of opposition from the community members around PLACE relates to author John Paul Lederach's idea of paradoxical curiosity from The Moral Imagination. Lederach explains paradoxical curiosity as "a permanent inquisitiveness that vigilantly explores the world of possibilities beyond the immediate arguments and narrow definitions of reality" (Lederach, 2010, pg. 37). He is essentially saying that paradoxical curiosity is looking beyond the obvious, looking beyond what we see right in front of us, to more clearly see the bigger picture of a situation. This outlook is important when looking at something like the role of a Purple Sea Urchin, but it is essential when looking at leadership for social justice. One way paradoxical curiosity can be practiced is through listening to voices across the spectrum of support, including the critical voices and those in opposition. As PLACE is attempting to include voices and opinions across the support spectrum in order to get the biggest picture possible, these voices of the opposition are ones that they are especially interested in.

The process of finding the voice of the opposition of PLACE was not an easy one for me. Eventually, I was able to find someone with concerns about PLACE. He responded to an email with the link to a petition against PLACE he had made three years ago on change.org, addressed to the mayor of St. Louis Park. While the petition hadn't been active for the past two years, I was surprised to see that 185 individuals had signed it. The petition itself had four main points of concern: increased traffic, unfinished light rail, safety of residents, and lack of funding. However, the comments of those who signed, as well as the follow up information posted by the man who started the petition, held a wide variety of concerns. These concerns included issues such as devalued housing, major building shade, and an anticipated stench from the anaerobic digester PLACE is so excited about. Because the spectrum of concerns span such a wide variety of people, I decided to attempt to make a single story out of the many voices on the petition in the form of a letter. This is a letter from a fictional character that has a fictional story, however it synthesizes real concerns from St. Louis Park community members. It is a letter from "The concerned community member."

To whom it may concern,

I have lived in St. Louis Park for over a decade in the Elmwood neighborhood directly next to where PLACE is building their new hotel and apartments. I have neighbors that have lived here much longer than I, as well as some that have just moved here. I am writing this letter because I care deeply about my neighbors, Elmwood neighborhood, and the St. Louis Park community in general. As PLACE begins to break ground near my house, I wanted to bring to light some of the concerns my neighbors and I have about this new development.

One of the main concerns of having a new apartment building and hotel being built in this area is the increase in traffic it will bring. There are already multiple apartment buildings, including a senior living apartment, as well as businesses and restaurants. The building of PLACE will surely bring more traffic from hotel business and cause troubles with parking for residents and business patrons. I do not want hotel-stayers or PLACE residents to be parking on my neighborhood streets. Along with parking issues, I am positive this development will increase traffic density in general. My commute to and from work is already long and frustrating enough, especially at the intersection at Wooddale Avenue and 36th Street, right next to where the new buildings are going up. I don't want to have to wait in even more traffic on my way home after a long day of work. Additionally, both my kids and the neighborhood kids like to walk/bike to school, the park or community center to play and the increased traffic will make it very dangerous for them to do so! PLACE is saying that they are hoping to mitigate this traffic problem with the usage of the new South West Light Rail. While I think this is a great idea, I don't think it is reasonable to believe that the new PLACE residents won't have their own cars. This is simply not going to be the case. It is so hard to get around the cities without a car. Yes, it is doable, but not likely. On top of this, the building of the South West Light Rail is going very slowly, so the first residents in PLACE will not even have the choice of using the system. These new apartments and hotel will undoubtedly bring more traffic to the area around my neighborhood causing a multitude of problems.

Another concern I have with the new development is the elements of PLACE itself. First, it is a big development that will not only take up a lot of space, but it will tower over other buildings around it. One of my friends has a one-story building that her family has owned for 40 years and the height of the new six-story buildings will shade it immensely. It feels like a lack of respect towards the long-standing community members. However, the size of the building is not the only problem. PLACE is planning on installing an aerobic digester on its property to supposedly make energy from waste. While this idea may be a good one in theory, in practice it is not as glamorous. In my research, I found that communities that have these digesters in them complain about a rancid trash smell that is filling their community. I absolutely do not want this to happen. My kids love playing outside and this would greatly affect their ability or desire to do this. This could also devalue my house because no one wants to live in a neighborhood that stinks like trash. Moreover, PLACE has been lacking in clarity about its financial situation as well as where its permit stands. I don't believe that they have properly checked off all the boxes before they started working.

Some community members are concerned about the types of people PLACE's mixed income housing will bring, as well as the abuse of low-income housing tax breaks, but the majority of the community is concerned about the increased traffic and the building itself which we believe will have a negative effect on the community. It does not seem to us like PLACE has been as diligent in permits, safety checks, and finances as they need to be, and-simply put - this is not a great place for a new development of apartments and a hotel. I take pride in my neighborhood and my home and I am in opposition to anything that would negatively impact and devalue those things. My neighbors and my community are important to me and this is why I wanted to voice my concern. I hope you will take into account these concerns because this project will affect my community (Wells).

Sincerely,
A Concerned St. Louis Park Community Member

PLACE is stepping into a role of leadership in the way of equitable and sustainable housing. As I have learned throughout my semester in our Leadership for Social Justice Class, there is not simply one definition of what a leader is. Leaders come in all forms, abilities, and personality types. However, there are a few characteristics that good leaders share, one of which is the ability to seriously listen and consider perspectives from the entire spectrum of support on an issue.

PLACE can take on this important leadership characteristic through Lederach's idea of paradoxical curiosity. Because the people at PLACE want to have a positive impact on the community of St. Louis Park, they must be willing to not only listen but to sincerely consider the things said by voices across the entire spectrum of support. As an organization, they have stated some of the promises they make to their future residents. One of these is a promise to develop "[r]obust networks with broader community of St. Louis Park and partner organizations so that residents have access to services that extend beyond their home" (welcometoplace.org). This community includes businesses and restaurants in the area, but also the residents who live near the site. Many of these residents have their own perspectives about PLACE, some of which are in opposition. Lederach would not see these concerned voices as wrong or dangerous, he would see them as pieces of the broader picture that may have been missed before. The voices of concerned community members are not necessarily wrong, just different. As much as PLACE wants to make a positive impact on the community of St. Louis park, they need to see the biggest picture possible, and they will do this best by looking to all who are interested and concerned.

As PLACE strives to be a leader in sustainable and equitable housing, they can use this idea of paradoxical curiosity. It is important as community-oriented leaders that they look beyond the obvious and beyond what is right in front of them. They can do this by listening to the voices of their opposition and voices outside the norm. Practically, this could look like regular forums where community members are invited to share their voice. Or perhaps it is an open-door policy for those developing PLACE to give access to community members who want to express their concerns. Creating even small ways to open spaces for dialogue is important for leaders as they attempt to serve communities and do effective social justice work. These voices should be valued and considered as they speak to the range of perspectives in the community. Just as the kelp forests need the prickly sea urchins to keep the ecosystem healthy, effective social justice leadership needs the voices of opposition to hear important perspectives and to keep the community healthy.

Works cited:

Lederach, J. P. (2010). The moral imagination: the art and soul of building peace. Oxford: Oxford University Press.

Pearse, J. (2006). Ecological Role of Purple Sea Urchins Science, 314(5801), 940-941. Retrieved from www.jstor.org/stable/20032771

The #AllThrive Campaign. (n.d.). Retrieved December 12, 2019, from www.welcometoplace.org/the_allthrive_campaign.

Wells, P. (n.d.). Sign the Petition. Retrieved December 14, 2019, from www.change.org/p/updated-petition-provide-the-place-project-schedule-project-updates.

About the Author – Katrina Anderson

I am a student at the University of St. Thomas majoring in Biology of Global Health and minoring in Justice and Peace Studies. While I do not know what I will be doing after I am done with school, I am passionate about working towards justice in the healthcare system. I also love to travel so hopefully I will be able to explore the world, too!

Community Housing

"In a consumer society contentment is a radical proposition. Recognizing abundance rather than scarcity undermines an economy that thrives by creating unmet desires. Gratitude cultivates an ethic of fullness, but the economy needs emptiness"
–Robin Wall Kimmerer

"Housing is core. It is a basic need in life, fundamental, and I don't think we appreciate it as much as we should. Many people do not have housing and it's essentially a platform to shape what our lives could be," she said.

For Gretchen, housing plays an important role in both her personal and professional life. Personally, she identifies as a white woman and a single parent, which brings its own set of housing needs. Although important, Gretchen sees housing as something bigger than just personal, for her it's systemic.

"My identity creates my ideas of what's important in the world," said Gretchen. "You're often running into people who have different ideas of what's important, and so part of my recognition is that communities are full of different values and beliefs. I know many of us focus on what we all hold the same, but there are also real differences. This tension or conflict is very much a part of how communities decide to do things."

Professionally, Gretchen works as a program officer for Local Initiatives Support Corporation in the Twin Cities. LISC is one of the largest organizations supporting projects to revitalize communities and bring greater economic opportunity to residents.

Gretchen stated that through her job she is working to create and preserve housing. (LISC Twin Cities)

"We are on the finance side. Financing is the mechanism by which housing is created, stabilized, and sustained. Through this role I work with communities to figure out what kinds of housing they want around them, and what does this kind of housing mean. Is there a kind of housing that is scary for them? Is there a kind of housing in which they envision their communities?"

There are many challenges involving housing in the Twin Cities, and many social justice issues that need to be addressed. At the forefront of these issues is racial inequality. In our communities, we need to assess and understand how institutional, systemic, and interpersonal racism play a role in housing. Certain biases and privilege can shield individuals from these racial housing issues, and ultimately, issues that play a role in deciding who gets to live where.

"There is a lot of 'othering' in our communities. That they aren't us, they don't belong here. There is a lot of biases about who is us," said Gretchen.

To address the social justice issues that are intertwined within the role housing plays in our communities, it's necessary to understand why housing is important. When asked to explain why housing is important to her, Gretchen explained that it is critical to know people who are housing vulnerable and be able to understand the stresses and challenges that being housing vulnerable creates for them.

"I spend time volunteering at a homeless shelter and have gotten to appreciate how preeminent being housing vulnerable is, and who these people are. This is tragic. Your heart cannot absorb all of it, it's very hard," said Gretchen. "In the work I do, I work a lot with advocates and people who support and council families who are in these vulnerable positions."

It is one step to gain an understanding of the importance of housing, it is another step to take action. Gretchen explained that one of the most influential ways to address these housing issues is for people to stand up and speak out about what they believe is important in their communities.

"What happens is that the loudest voices are always the people who are the most afraid, and the people with the greatest fear always win. The ones who are the most afraid are going to have the most limitations on what kinds of housing they want, and they end up dominating and constricting the whole community," said Gretchen. "I wish we could hold each other accountable to the whole community, but for some reason we're afraid to do that."

When asked what she wished was different about housing in the Twin Cities, Gretchen replied simply with, "Oh, there are a lot of things." But one concept she is increasingly sensitive towards is how housing in our society is viewed as a commodity.

"We've put a value on housing and that value is intended to create our wealth, and our wealth, in a capitalistic society, is very individualistic. We are all about getting more for us as individuals and we have less compassion and concern for the broader communities' wealth," she said.

In other words, the more concerned people are becoming with their individual wealth, the less concerned they are about the wealth of the community as a whole. This in turn leads to less focus on community success and creating achievement together, and more emphasis on individual success. Gretchen pointed out that it's not only the wealthy who have taken this approach, it is also the low-income population.

"Everyone wants to be a part of that American dream, they want to have that security of comfort and that sense of arrival in terms of 'this is my world and I can control it'." she added. With housing being viewed as a commodity in our society, we are also making it disposable. Commodities are made to last only a short period of time. It is all very wasteful, and housing is a contributor.

"Increasingly, we are making housing as a kind of throw away. We don't make things last beyond 15 years typically. We think okay, well in 15 years we will do something else," said Gretchen. "It is a very 'throw away' like mentality that is driven by just trying to make a quick buck and not really caring about the long-term prospects."

Approaching these concerns regarding housing can be difficult. The concept of housing as a commodity is ever present in our society, and most are focused on advancing their individual wealth. Thoughts and ideas regarding community wealth and success are usually put on the back burner, if they are even thought about at all.

In her book, Braiding Sweetgrass, Robin Wall Kimmerer approaches the issue of commoditized housing in our communities, and commoditized economy as a whole, by suggesting that the nature of objects can change depending on how that object comes to us.

Robbin Wall Kimmerer is a mother, scientist, decorated professor, and enrolled member of the Citizen Potawatomi Nation. She is SUNY Distinguished Teaching Professor of Environmental Biology and the founder and director of the Center for Native Peoples and the Environment. Kimmerer (2013) states, "It's funny how the nature of an object – let's say a strawberry or a pair of socks – is so changed by the way it has come into your hands, as a gift or as a commodity" (p. 26). She goes on to further explain that if that pair of socks is bought at the store as a commodity, the buyer has no inherent obligation to those socks, and the reciprocity between buyer and seller ends at the exchange of currency. But if those exact socks were received as a gift, it will create an ongoing relationship of reciprocity. "As the scholar and writer Lewis Hyde notes, 'It is the cardinal difference between gift and commodity exchange that a gift establishes a feeling-bond between two people'" (p. 26), says Kimmerer (2013).

But how can changing the way an object is obtained help address the issues of commoditized housing in our communities? "This is hard to grasp for societies steeped in notions of private property, where others are, by definition, excluded from sharing," (p. 27) says Kimmerer (2019). She explains that in a commoditized, private property economy, gifts are deemed to be free because one does not exchange currency to obtain it. But gifts in the gift economy are not free. "The essence of the gift is that it creates a set of relationships. The currency of a gift economy is, at its root, reciprocity. In Western thinking, private land is understood to be a 'bundle of rights,' whereas in a gift economy property has a 'bundle of responsibilities attached" (Kimmerer, 2013, p. 28). Commoditizing housing leaves people out – leaves people without homes. If the viewpoint of housing in our communities shifts from a commodity to a gift, it creates an emphasis on responsibility to relationships in that community, bringing people together instead of separating people from others. Then, one is not solely sustained from individual wealth, but they can also grow through the relationships and responsibilities of their community.

PLACE, the housing development in Saint Louis Park, Minnesota, is trying to change the housing narrative in the Twin Cities. They want to emphasize community wealth and togetherness as a whole, instead of focusing on individual wealth. Throughout PLACE's development process, they have been holding multiple community wide meetings to cultivate relationships, collaboration, and ideas. As a change-making housing development, PLACE could not achieve all their goals without a strong community backing (Welcome to PLACE). As Kimmerer (2013) said, "We can choose. If all the world is a commodity, how poor we grow. When all the world is a gift in motion, how wealthy we become" (p. 31)

Works Cited

Kimmerer, Robin. Braiding Sweetgrass. Milkweed Editions, 2013.

"About Us - Staff." LISC Twin Cities, www.lisc.org/twin-
    cities/about-us/staff/. Accessed 2019.

"PLACE." Welcome to PLACE, www.welcometoplace.org/slp.
    Accessed 2019.

About the Author – Maria Golberg

I am in my fourth year at the University of St. Thomas majoring in Business Management and minoring in Sustainability and Justice and Peace Studies. In my free time you can find me reading, creating art, or spending time with loved ones. I am humbled to be a part of this project, and to promote positive social change.

Community

Creating Home

As I walk into 729 N Washington Ave, Minneapolis, I am surprised by the perfectly situated lobby, filled with all kinds of pleasing geometric shapes, lines, and curves. I'm even greeted by the warm aromas of a coffee shop as I push past the bulky front doors. Situated in North Loop, I begin to imagine the kinds of people who call this office building home for 8-12 hours a day. This place is contemporary, cool, and seems way out of my price point. I walk to the elevators near the back, let out a nervous-excited exhale, and show myself up to 'Suite 600' on the sixth floor of the building. I experience instant sensory overload walking into "We Work", an office space of "creators, leaders, and self-starters (WeWork)."

WeWork is a sleek, multi-leveled office-space I feel like I've seen before in romantic comedies that take place in New York City. It is clear why PLACE, the innovative nonprofit filled with folks who want to challenge the status quo of housing, picked this space to set up shop, work, and create. I pick a large, brightly colored chair, and send the message, "Hi Alice, I just arrived here on the 6th floor, what a cool space! I'm in a grey and purple St. Thomas sweatshirt. I'm waiting in some funky orange chairs! See you soon." Moments later, Alice walks through the door and offers me a drink. Putting a face to a name I had been email corresponding with for the first time was refreshing. She's just as kind and inviting as I had thought. My choices are kombucha, cold press coffee, or water, all from a tap.

I'm most curious about the kombucha, so I grab a glass and head up to the top floor to get settled.

As we begin to converse, the story of Alice Hiniker begins to unravel. I did my research on Alice and her background and find that her passion for equity and healthy homes matches up with everything I had found online. Alice is one of the architects on the PLACE team, who has a devotion to sustainability in new and existing buildings, as well as a drive to create living environments deeply rooted in community that are accessible to people regardless of their financial or personal situation. These values developed throughout Alice's younger years, her academic career and into her professional one, graduating with her Bachelor of Science in Architecture at the University of Michigan in 2009, and becoming LEED AP BD+C in that same year.

Volunteering is a value that has been close to Alice's heart all of her life since she was young, so offering her time at Greenbuild during 2009 and 2010 came naturally to her. She laughs as she tells the story about discovering PLACE, "I showed up and they told me they can't hire me, and I said, 'Well what if I start showing up for free?'... Even if you won't pay me, I want to be a part of this... since no one else is doing what PLACE is doing."

Alice has been with PLACE for 5 years now and has been learning lessons of home and a sense of belonging along the way. Since Alice will be creating homes for many people at PLACE, I'm curious to know what home means to her. Her answers paint an image of home in my mind, one that smells like paper and crisp air, and is filled with close-knit relationships. Alice says that to her, home is a concept that has gradually evolved over time. It is place she can comfortably read a good book, have access to rich natural spaces, be around those she loves and have a strong sense of belonging. She says that creating a space of connection and family is a goal she has when thinking about designing future homes at PLACE. "A big part of that is not just the location but the environment in which we're living," She says, "Which means feeling like the place we're in is our own, not just somewhere we're renting for a short period of time and then leaving."

She says that although renting an apartment presents natural barriers to creating home, a goal of PLACE is to be as flexible as possible when allowing residents to design their own space. They also want to create opportunities for residents to express themselves, which looks like putting a wall of chalkboard paint in each apartment and incorporating interactive art, such as light projection art by local artists into shared community spaces. However, Alice knows from her own experience that sometimes there aren't incentives for transforming a space one knows is temporary. She explains that PLACE's idea to incentivize people to create a space that feels like their own, is to compensate those who add shelves, storage units, or other personal touches to their spaces. This idea, she says, will help residents feel like they'll maintain the benefit of putting work into their space, even if they're only there for a short period of time.

I notice through Alice's personal stories, the attention to detail and engagement with community partners that sustainability and housing equity are at the forefront of Alice and the rest of the team's goals for PLACE. "She recognizes that diversity is what makes a community whole, something she will be paying attention to as she transitions from living in her home in the Twin Cities and moves back to her smaller hometown in Michigan. She sees the work being done at PLACE, including neighborhood-scale renewable energy and obtaining housing vouchers to insure more living opportunities are available despite one's income, as the future of housing that we all should be demanding from development companies.

After about an hour and 15 minutes that was only intended to be 45, Alice gives me a tour of the PLACE team's office and invites me to take a self-guided tour of the common spaces I didn't see. I think she's picked up on my enthusiasm about the office, and I gladly stroll between floors before I see myself back to the main floor. As I peer into the fishbowl looking conference rooms contained by glass walls and notice the vegan snacks available at the front desk, I reflect on the playing field of privilege, access and opportunity the PLACE team is trying to even out in their creation of community. The starting price for a "Hot Desk" at WeWork is $300/mo., giving access to a chair and a shared table space, and going up to $500/mo. for a private office (WeWork). I think about myself, as a lower-middle class white student about to graduate from undergrad, and the slim possibility of having financial access to a space like this should I want to create a startup. I think about how that possibility slims for soon-to-be graduates from marginalized communities my same age, other women, and those in lower socioeconomic classes than I am. I consider further how the opportunity to work in this space slims more and more as I remove privileges, like access to higher education, quality high school education, and access to healthy food, health care and living spaces.

In Chimamanda Ngozi Adichie's TED Talk, "A Danger of a Single Story," Adichie addresses the dangers that come along with a single narrative guiding one's perception of someone or something. In her talk, she explains that basing one's knowledge of a group of people, a system, or an ideology limits the wide range of experiences within them. Adichie notes that we are unable to talk about single stories without talking about power, and who has the power to tell stories in what way. She says:

> The Palestinian poet Mourid Barghouti writes that if you want to dispossess a people, the simplest way to do it is to tell their story, and to start with, "secondly." Start the story with the arrows of the Native Americans, and not with the arrival of the British, and you have and entirely different story. Start the story with the failure of the African state, and

not with the colonial creation of the African state, and you
have an entirely different story.

The single-story being presented to housing consumers limits us to
what we can and cannot ask for when it comes to creating
community in sustainable and equitable spaces. It skips past histories
of generational and economic trauma resulting from stolen land,
housing covenants, and redlining; It skips forward to telling us that
access to beautiful, healthy living spaces is only for those who have
the right privileges to afford it. It tells us that we must fit into the
box being presented, and if we can't do that, we can't live in the
apartment complex, townhome community, housing development,
etc. Through work done by Alice and the rest of the team, PLACE is
challenging the status quo and is showing it is possible to create an
eco-community where all are welcome and celebrated and can live in
a way that will enhance the future for all of us.

"What keeps me coming back is it's not just about this
project in St. Louis Park, it's about saying this type of project is
possible," Alice said, "And so we need to keep making these, we
need to push for these, we need to ask for more. We can't keep
accepting the conventional box of everything." My time spent with
Alice leaves me hopeful, challenged, and inspired for the future of
what housing can and should be. She helped me to see that creating
home is more than building 4 walls and a ceiling, but is shifting the
control of who is telling the story of housing and creating
opportunities for all to be welcomed with open arms.

Works Cited:
Adichie C. N. (2009). The Danger of a Single Story. TED Talk
Velasco, C., & Hiniker, A. (2019). PLACE. Retrieved from
      https://www.welcometoplace.org
WeWork. (2019). Retrieved from https://www.wework.com/.

About the Author – Madeline Harvey

I was named by my mother (a kindergarten teacher) after the classic children's book about the little French girl in a yellow coat, however, I usually go by 'Maddie'. "Home" to me has looked like a blue-grey colored house on Daniels St. in southern Minnesota, a welcoming homestay near the shores of Durban, South Africa, and spunky college homes on both sides of Marshall Ave in St. Paul. I will be graduating in the Spring of 2020 with her Bachelor of Arts and Sciences degree in Communication and Journalism and Justice and Peace Studies. I plan to attend grad school and find ways to incorporate values learned in undergrad of creating community, critically analyzing unjust systems and challenging the status quo in my vocation. Things that make me feel the most alive include, trying new food in different cities, spending the day with my grandma and connecting with the divine through reading, meditation, and laughing with the bright souls around me.

Finding a Home and Community for the Arts

Abandoned warehouses, closed schools, old factories. What do you think of when you see these places? Some would say damaged dreams or lost opportunities. But artists see something different. Big rooms for workspaces, concrete floors that can get dirty with paint or paper mache, and large windows that provide plenty of natural light. This is what Jessica Turtle explained to me as we met for coffee in early November.

Jessica is a board member for PLACE, becoming interested in PLACE because of their involvement in artist housing. Jessica has spent her life as an artist, graduating from the University of Wisconsin with a Fine Arts degree in Metal Fabrication and a minor in Sociology. As a result, she has also spent most of her adult life in artist housing.

Artist housing is naturally a dual-purpose space; for living and for work. Because commercial spaces have expensive rent, artist tend to combine work and home. Both of these needs must be met. Artists generally prefer large concrete rooms with plenty of natural lighting for their creative process, and as a result, most artist housing tends to be older industrial buildings and schools (Turtle, Jessica, personal communication, November 8, 2019). In the United States, most artist housing programs follow similar models to one another. The model is affordable but comes with some challenges as well.

Jessica explained these models, noting that first, tenants must be artists or part of the art industry: Performing artists, Visual artists, writers, or art administrators to name a few. Artists must make below a certain income, in general around $40,000. A lot of artist housing uses a cooperative model, where potential tenants must meet and be approved by everyone living in the building. As a final piece, most artist housing models requires artists to leave their homes open to the public (Turtle, Jessica, personal communication, November 8, 2019). No other industry in the US requires you to give up your privacy, which makes this final piece especially challenging. Jessica, who spent most of her 20s living in artist housing in places like Duluth, Chicago and the Twin Cities, has seen this model in every city she has lived in (Turtle, Jessica, personal communication, November 8, 2019).

PLACE's model changes this aspect. The organization plans on offering two types of live/work spaces for artists. The first type models what most artist living spaces look like today, with natural lighting and large spaces (PLACE, 2019). PLACE's second model offers creative's a smaller commercial space (PLACE, 2019). When it comes to showing their craft, artists do not need large storefronts. PLACE plans to create units with smaller storefronts at the front of the unit and private living areas near the back (PLACE, 2019).

The community within artist housing represents another important aspect of artist housing, but developing this community presents a tall task. One example of building community can be found in Paducah, Kentucky, where the city started their own artist relocation program as a way to attract artists to their area. The program started from the combined efforts of local artists and city planners and resulted in the creation of an arts-based culture in Paducah's Lowertown (Artist Relocation Program. 2015.). The program continues to attract artists to the city and has made Paducah a travel destination for those interested in the arts. The artists within Paducah feel the strength of the community. One local artist referred to it as the "perfect storm," noting that the "energized community" and its closeness to Paducah's "delightful downtown" has led over

70 artists to move there, many from out of state (Daniel, D. 2007.). Building a community is necessary to attract and retain creatives.

Jessica admits that creating an artist community can be a difficult process. "You are asking a bunch of very eccentric individuals to all live together and work together" (Turtle, Jessica, personal communication, November 8, 2019). But she notes the value of building a collaborative community. "You are meeting your network. You are living next door to your network" (Turtle, Jessica, personal communication, November 8, 2019). Ultimately, these communities attracted her to artist housing. The communities contained individuals with passion for their own crafts, and their passion drove and motivated her to push herself as an artist. Most people identify with this feeling that Jessica expressed. We want to surround ourselves with communities that push us to do our best. We surround ourselves with people that have the qualities that we want to see in ourselves. When artists and artist housing programs put in hard work to build a supportive and motivated community, the community as a whole is bound to be successful.

About the Author - Andrew Miller

I am a student studying Environmental Studies, Geographic Information Systems, and Education. I hold environmental justice close to my heart, and I am intrigued by the way art can influence how we think and interact with the environment. I believe that everything in life is connected, and I hope this book illustrates how our relationships to the environment, housing, art, and ultimately one another can serve as the building blocks to a sustainable future.

Works Cited:

Artist Relocation Program. (2015). Retrieved from
http://www.paducahmainstreet.org/artist-relocation-program.htm

Daniel, D. (2007). Art community thrives in a Kentucky river
        town. The Boston Globe, 1-2. Retrieved from
        http://archive.boston.com/travel/getaways/us/articles/2007/
        10/28/art_community_thrives_in_a_kentucky_river_town/?
        page=1
"St. Louis Park, Minnesota." PLACE, 2019,
        www.welcometoplace.org/slp.
Turtle, Jessica, personal communication, November 8, 2019

The Geography of St. Louis Park

The story of the modern landscape of St. Louis Park begins roughly 12,000 years ago, when the last of the Laurentide ice sheet covered central Minnesota. When this ice sheet retreated, it left behind over a hundred of feet of sediment in some places, a mostly flat landscape, and depressions in the land that became the lakes that current residents of the metro treasure. As Minnesota began to experience a warmer climate, the state split into four distinct ecological biomes. St. Louis Park is located in the Eastern Broadleaf Forest Province (Minnesota DNR). This biome serves as a transition between the western portion of the state that is historically prairie, and the coniferous forests of northeast Minnesota. The Eastern Broadleaf Forest Province features hardwoods such as oaks, maples, hickories, and basswood. This landscape brought lumber baron Thomas Barlow Walker to St Louis Park in 1890, who began developing St Louis Park for industrial, commercial and residential use.

Today St Louis Park is a bustling suburb with a growing population of almost 50,000 (U.S. Census Bureau). With St Louis Parks' growing population, the city needs to consider how to meet both the needs of the community and mitigate the effects of climate change. Currently, single family homes make up over 83% of the housing in St Louis Park. This is not sustainable either environmentally or in terms of development because only 2% of the land in St Louis park remains vacant. As St Louis Park works towards a carbon neutral city in 2040, as proposed in their 2017

Climate Action Plan, an answer to the question of available and affordable housing and the environment may be the current multi-family, transit oriented, and sustainable development PLACE.

About the Author – Olivia Jascor

I am currently studying geology and environmental studies at the University of St Thomas. I spent most of my childhood running in the woods and playing on my grandparent's farm. This upbringing has made me passionate about preserving the Midwest's prairies and creating environmentally sustainable communities so others can enjoy the nature that I grew up with.

Works Cited:

"Deciduous Forest - Biomes of Minnesota - Minnesota DNR." Minnesota Department of Natural Resources, www.dnr.state.mn.us/biomes/deciduous.html.

"U.S. Census Bureau QuickFacts: St. Louis Park City, Minnesota; United States." Census Bureau QuickFacts, www.census.gov/quickfacts/fact/table/stlouisparkcityminnes ota,US/PST045218.

A Contaminated Past

PLACE is entering the community of St. Louis Park with ambitious goals focusing on sustainability. This includes goals to cut carbon emissions and pollution, and to improve sustainable living practices. For example, PLACE will be implementing an e-generator that will turn food waste into energy as well as fertilizer for organic farming. They will also be using solar panels to charge electric cars, and they are strategically located on the expansion of the light rail into St. Louis Park. Moreover, they are planting a small urban forest to provide green space to residents, and they are located along a bike-trail, providing more outdoor space and options for alternative transportation (PLACE, 2019). It can clearly be seen that environmental protection and advocacy is at the forefront of thinking when it comes to PLACE and the community they are attempting to develop in St. Louis Park, but it hasn't always been that way with companies that operate in the city.

In the past, St. Louis Park has been a site of environmental contamination that has greatly affected the community. From 1917-1972 the company Reilly Tar and Chemical was located on an 80-acre site on the corner of Highway 7 and Louisiana Avenue South. This company was a coal tar distillation and creosote wood preserving plant, and due to the materials needed to do this work, the company created a lot of hazardous waste. The problem with this is that some of the waste was disposed of improperly, which caused it to leak into the groundwater system. Specifically, polycyclic aromatic hydrocarbons, or PAHs leaked into the groundwater. The city of St. Louis Park receives 100% of its drinking water from ground water, so when this was discovered years later, the city shut down 6 municipal drinking water wells from 1978-1979 and continues to treat the water for all contaminants today. The site was placed on the Environmental Protection Agency's National Priority List, which gave them additional resources to remediate the contamination as part of the federal superfund program (Minnesota Department of Health, 2016).

The closure of drinking water wells and the information that the groundwater had been contaminated caused concern for many residents of St. Louis Park, especially those that lived and grew up near the Reilly Tar and Chemical site. A lot of this concern stemmed from the lack of information provided to the residents for many years. Due to the lack of information, residents were often left to fill in the blanks with their concerns and fears. For example, around 2015, a Facebook group titled "St. Louis Park Cancer Cluster/Reilly Tar Superfund Site" was created, and it now has almost 1600 members. Many of the stories posted on this page include individuals who have been affected by cancer or neurological disorders or who have neighbors or family members who have been affected, and the site even includes a map of documented cases of cancer or neurological disorders within St. Louis Park that have been shared on the page. Along with the Facebook page, the widespread coverage of the water contamination crisis in Flint, Michigan has sparked an increase in concern for the water quality, as well as an increase in the distrust residents have for local, state, and federal officials providing information on this topic (Reinan, 2016).

On the other side of this, the St. Louis Park city government has recently, in October 2016, released a more extensive report detailing the groundwater contamination and the clean-up efforts. Some concerns were also addressed with a study done by Minnesota

Department of Health, which found that the cancer rate in St. Louis Park between 1993-2012 was average for the metro area. Although, residents have responded to this saying that this study does not include individuals who grew up in St. Louis Park and have since left, and it does include individuals who have recently moved into the community and have not been exposed to the contamination, making the results more average than they really are. The uncertainty of this has affected many of the past and present residents of St. Louis Park, and although more information is available now than in the past, there is still feelings of concern and distrust (Reinan, 2016).

To add to the concern residents of St. Louis Park have about their drinking water, in 2004 it was discovered that a site on the opposite corner of Highway 7 and Louisiana Avenue South, across from the Reilly Tar and Chemical site, had been contaminating ground water with vinyl chloride, which can cause kidney and liver problems (Minnesota Department of Health, 2016). This site, like the Reilly Tar and Chemical site, has requested to become a part of the National Priorities List, but has not yet been accepted. This would allow the Minnesota Pollution Control Agency to investigate further who caused the groundwater contamination as part of the federal superfund program (Klecker, 2019). Again, residents were concerned for their health, although unlike the Reilly Tar and Chemical site, there has not been as much speculation about the effects of this, such as a Facebook group. This may be because information about the contamination and remediation process was more readily available to residents, or because the contamination occurred more recently, and the possibility of long-term effects has yet to be seen. In both of these cases, the groundwater contamination occurred in middle-class neighborhoods of mostly single-family homes, where the average home value ranges from $100,000 to $250,000 (Maxfield Research and Consulting, 2018).

St. Louis Park is a city that has very aggressive and optimistic plans for the future of their impact on the environment, and this can be seen in PLACE as well, but the city has a long history of pollution that is still affecting the community today. In this history, it can be seen how important transparency can be in times of uncertainty. It can also be seen how members of the community work to create change through strategies on the social change wheel. The social change wheel is a diagram of seven ways one can enact social change. This wheel includes grassroots political activity/public policy work, confrontational strategies, voting/formal political activities, community economic development, charitable volunteerism, community building, and education. With a diverse array of actions one can take, the wheel shows how easy it can be to participate in social change in one way or another (University of St. Thomas Justice and Peace Studies, 2016).

Looking at the groundwater contamination that has occurred in St. Louis Park, the social change wheel is useful to show options on how to create lasting change. The punishment of a company for causing contamination may deter that company from committing further contamination, but to create lasting change for the city as a whole, broader social change must occur. One way that has already been seen is the grassroots organizing done using the Facebook group, "St. Louis Park Cancer Cluster/Reilly Tar Superfund Site". This site has brought together almost 1600 members to build a community against further groundwater contamination, and to bring a skeptical eye to the remediation and informational processes. This brought about change when, after much request, the city of St. Louis Park released further information about the contamination and remediation processes.

The social change wheel has also been used by PLACE, during their efforts to improve environmental sustainability and in building their community. One way this can be seen is through community economic development. In their community they have invested in renewable resources for energy and are they building with sustainable practices in mind. It is also evident through their investment in an urban forest, providing the surrounding community with outdoor space. They have also used education, community building, and political activity/public policy all in an effort to create a community driven to be more environmentally sustainable. The concept of the social change wheel is important for PLACE and the St. Louis Park community because it provides a path for anybody, regardless of time or interests, to participate in creating a cleaner and more sustainable St. Louis Park.

About the Author – Brooke Hudrlik

I am currently a senior at the University of St. Thomas, majoring in Environmental Studies and minoring in Spanish and Geology. I am passionate about environmental sustainability, and after graduation I hope to begin working in this field. In my free time I enjoy cooking and doing anything outside.

Works Cited:

Klecker, M. (2019, November 1). EPA proposes putting polluted site in St. Louis Park and Edina into Superfund program. Retrieved from http://www.startribune.com/epa-proposes-putting-polluted-site-in-st-louis-park-and-edina-into-superfund-program/564194332/.

Maxfield Research and Consulting, LLC. (2018). Comprehensive housing Market Study Update for the City of St. Louis Park, Minnesota. Comprehensive housing Market Study Update for the City of St. Louis Park, Minnesota. Retrieved from https://www.stlouispark.org/home/showdocument?id=11949

Minnesota Department of Health, Environmental Health Division. (2016). St. Louis Park Drinking Water. St. Louis Park Drinking Water. Retrieved from

https://www.health.state.mn.us/communities/environment/ha
zardous/docs/sites/hennepin/slpdwrepup0117.pdf

PLACE. (n.d.). Retrieved November 20, 2019, from
https://www.welcometoplace.org/.

Reinan, J. (2016, May 7). Cancer fears fester over St. Louis Park
Superfund site. Retrieved November 20, 2019, from
http://www.startribune.com/cancer-fears-fester-in-st-louis-
park/378526645/?refresh=true.

University of St. Thomas, Minnesota Justice and Peace Studies.
(2016, June 28). Retrieved from
https://www.stthomas.edu/justpeace/academics/.

Rethinking Approaches to
Housing and Food Insecurity

Housing insecurity is an extremely intersectional problem that spreads across communities and affects people in many different ways. When housing became more affordable after World War II, people, predominantly white, began to move out into the more desirable suburbs. The jobs slowly followed the rush of people out of the urban areas. This left many individuals and families stranded without the financial means to make it by. As wealthy people began to move out of the suburbs, the average income in the cities decreased. From this, nearly half of the grocery stores closed in the cities due to the lack of purchasing power (Walker, 2010). This left many individuals and families in a state of food insecurity. One large problem that contributes to housing insecurity is the impact of food deserts. They are classified as areas where it is difficult to buy and access affordable healthy foods. Food deserts are rooted in socioeconomic problems, and were initiated through economic segregation in the 1970s and 1980s (Walker, 2010). This further shows that this is an issue that disproportionately affects people who are experiencing poverty, have limited access to vehicles and transportation, and people who haven't had access to higher education. In addition, we can see the impacts on areas experiencing food insecurity through income, 40-48 percent lower, home values, 58-69 percent lower, and poverty rates 3 times higher (Singh, 2003).

Perhaps one of the main contributors to food insecurity is the lack of income after paying for other essential expenses. After paying for shelter costs, such as rent and utilities, many poor and near poor households become "shelter poor", meaning that they have little discretionary income left to pay for other crucial needs such as food (Coleman-Jensen, 2017). The significance of shelter can be seen as people experiencing poverty prioritize housing over other human needs. With the lack of funds, people experiencing poverty are already pushed into worse living, education, and overall health conditions that in return increase the poverty gap and promote the cycle of inequality. People who are in this situation essentially have to decide for themselves and their families, what is important enough for them to spend money on. In this case, there are things that will be left out such as healthy foods and education. This further emphasizes the strain that is put on communities that are experiencing poverty and food insecurity, but there are people and organizations who are working to combat it.

Edgar Rudberg, Ph.D. in natural sciences and management, gave his insights on housing insecurity through a personal interview. His background as an entrepreneur, who made little money starting up, allowed him to experience and observe the impacts of housing insecurity across the nation. He lived along the coasts in Miami, San Francisco and has had family in LA. These locations are arguably some of the most housing insecure places in the country. One of the main factors that amplified unaffordable housing is the disproportionate increase in living cost compared to wage increase. As a result, people experiencing poverty end up spending the majority of their checks on housing costs, which leaves little room for other expenses such as education, health care, and healthy foods. Rudberg acknowledged the intersectionality of issues surrounding affordable housing and argued that one of the main ways to combat the issue is by addressing systematic poverty. Additionally, he emphasized the need for healthy and affordable foods for children. Rudberg stated, "If we want our children to grow up and become successful and educated, we need healthy food in their bellies that will allow them to learn and grow." A way to promote healthy foods throughout the community is to be sustainable on multiple levels. These include obtaining healthy foods locally, turning food waste into energy, and attempting to lower the cost of living for members in the community.

The organization PLACE, a mixed-use, mixed-income, transit-oriented community demonstrating profound environmental design, is doing just that. In addition to mixed housing, PLACE is creating 119 jobs. Some jobs are specifically for people living onsite, and others provide studio spaces for people who have creative jobs (PLACE, 2019). Allowing jobs to be created on sight will continue to help combat housing insecurity. Rudberg's role in the organization is through the E-Generation, a neighborhood-scale system that produces organic food and energy for the community. His main focus is to utilize compost and other organic waste that is made from the community and turn it into something useful. In this case, he is converting organic waste into energy, fertilizer, and heat for PLACE. The process of doing this is through anaerobic digestion. The Environmental Protection Agency describes anaerobic digestion as the natural process in which microorganisms break down organic matter in the absence of air, or an anaerobic environment (Frequent Questions about Anaerobic Digestion, 2016). The organization is hoping that E-energy will generate the majority of the project's energy from renewable sources and organic materials, as well as grow healthy food for the people locally. This is not only profitable for the community who will have access to affordable healthy food, but the cost of energy will dramatically decrease due to the fact that energy is being produced on site. This is a great first step to combating food deserts and implementing sustainable energy in our communities.

Rudberg believes that PLACE can be an example and catalyst for sustainable housing models for the future. He states, "This is an opportunity to look at housing and our food systems in a different way and make everything far more local." The first order is to show how sustainability and the private sector can be catalysts for change in the future. Through his business mindset, Rudberg identified a problem with sustainable solutions. There is a large presence telling people to go green and carbon neutral, but there are very few affordable alternatives. He believes that there needs to be more sustainable solutions available for the public. One example he shared was through Xcel Energy. He thought that they should offer clean energy alternatives such as bio based, solar, and renewable, for the consumers to choose. This is a perfect example of what PLACE is doing through anaerobic digestion and renewable natural gas. They are providing a sustainable source of energy for their consumers, and they are allowing them to decide which form of energy they want to consume. Even if it is at a higher price, it is going to catalyze the market, and there could potentially be anaerobic digestion flooding the marketplace. Rudberg believes that is a huge opportunity to change energy and agricultural systems. He also thinks that getting farmers and businesspeople to adopt and catalyze systems of compost in modern agriculture is another key component for the future. By involving the private sector to combat social norms and to move toward more sustainable housing and food sources, potential benefits could arise. This can consist of paying people a good living wage, still providing good jobs for people, and doing something good even for the environment. Furthermore, the opportunity to have affordable healthy foods and housing will allow people experiencing poverty to have more opportunities in the future that they may not have had in the past.

Rudberg speculates that educating the marketplace surrounding sustainable alternatives and giving them sustainable solutions is the key to making efficient, ethical and sustainable solutions for the future. If we allow consumers to see the benefits of choosing sustainable alternatives, then we will slowly see a shift away from energy that is detrimental to the environment. Although sustainability in housing still has a long way to go, it is important to see the potential in society and where we can improve. Myles Horton has a similar philosophy in his book The Long Haul:

> I like to think that I have two eyes that I don't have to use the same way. When I do educational work with a group of people, I try to see with one eye where those people are as they perceive themselves to be. I do this by looking at body language, by imagination, by talking to them, by visiting with them, by learning what they enjoy and what troubles them. I try to find out where they are, and if I can get a hold of that with one eye, that's where I start. You have to start where people are because their growth is going to be from there, not from some abstraction or where you are or someone else is. With my other eye, it wasn't a problem because I already knew the direction I'd like to see people moving (131)

This quote further emphasizes the importance of meeting people where they are at. If we ever want to reach solutions surrounding housing, we need to work together and trust in one another. If we continue to have such a divide throughout our community, progress will be hindered or potentially halted. We also need to understand that if there is going to be change, it will be gradual, but if we continue to have people like Edgar Rudberg, and organizations like PLACE, it will lead us one step closer to mitigating food and housing insecurity.

About the Author - Joey Benning

I am a student studying Environmental Studies and Geographic Information Systems at the University of Saint Thomas. I have a passion and drive for making sustainable change within myself and in the communities of which I am a part. I hope that this book can help promote change within communities and that it allows the narrative of housing and food insecurity to be seen in a different way.

Works Cited

Coleman-Jensen, A., Steffen, B., & Whitley, S. (2017). Food Insecurity and Housing Insecurity. In Tickamyer A., Sherman J., & Warlick J. (Eds.), Rural Poverty in the United States (pp. 257-298). NEW YORK: Columbia University Press. Retrieved from www.jstor.org/stable/10.7312/tick17222.17

Rudberg, Edgar, personal communication, November 15, 2019

Frequent Questions about Anaerobic Digestion. (2016, October 3). Retrieved November 10, 2019, from https://www.epa.gov/anaerobic-digestion/frequent-questions-about-anaerobic-digestion.

Horton, Myles. (1998). The Long Haul: An Autobiography. New York, NY: Teacher College Press

Singh, G. K. (2003). Area deprivation and widening inequalities in US mortality, 1969–1998. American Journal of Public Health, 93(7), 1137-1143.

"St. Louis Park, Minnesota." PLACE, 2019, www.welcometoplace.org/slp.

Walker, R. E., Keane, C. R., & Burke, J. G. (2010). Disparities and access to healthy food in the united states: A review of food deserts literature. Health & Place, 16(5), 876-884.

St. Louis Park Climate Action Plan

In February of 2018 St Louis Park put out one of the most aggressive climate action plans in the nation. The city is looking to achieve net carbon neutrality by 2040. The city includes several ambitious targets to meet their goal. Based on PLACE's design plan and sustainability initiatives, they fit in perfectly with St Louis Parks visions for the future. St Louis Park includes seven goals in their Climate Action Plan:

1. Reduce energy consumption in large commercial and industrial buildings by 30% by 2030.
2. Reduce energy consumption in small to midsize commercial buildings by 30% by 2030.
3. By 2030 design all new construction to be net-zero energy.
4. Reduce energy consumption in residential buildings by 35% by 2030.
5. Achieve 100% renewable electricity by 2030.
6. Reduce vehicle emissions by 25% by 2030.
7. Achieve a 50% reduction in waste by 2030.

Implementation of these goals will result in a 55% reduction of greenhouse gas emissions by 2030, and 62% by 2040. With these goals in mind, PLACE's own sustainability initiates will help St Louis Park to achieve net carbon neutrality in 2040. PLACE holds a neighborhood patent for E-Generation. This program turns food waste into energy using anaerobic digestion. The carbon dioxide produced from this process will then be pumped into the on-site greenhouse, making this a closed system. This system will help St Louis Park's goal of reducing waste and reducing energy consumption in residential buildings. Another sustainability initiative is PLACE's dedication to reducing residents' reliance on vehicles. PLACE is located on the future Green Line light rail extension into Minneapolis, they are including electric vehicle charging stations, and including an urban forest bike path. This will help St Louis Park with their goal of reducing vehicle emissions by 25%.

Comparing St Louis Park's Climate Action Plan and PLACE's commitment to sustainability, it is clear why PLACE has found a home in St Louis Park. PLACE and St Louis Park can be a model for the rest of the country for how to implement sustainability within communities.

About the Author – Olivia Jascor

I am currently studying geology and environmental studies at the University of St Thomas. I spent most of my childhood running in the woods and playing on my grandparent's farm. This upbringing has made me passionate about preserving the Midwest's prairies and creating environmentally sustainable communities so others can enjoy the nature that I grew up with.

Works Cited

"Climate Action Plan" Retrieved March 05, 2020 from:
https://www.stlouispark.org/our-city/climate-action-plan

Paved Valued Space and Put Up a Parking Lot

*One reason [why] housing costs are so high is because
everybody's subsidizing the parking, especially parking garages,
with a higher rent. Parking is expensive from a space cost as well
a construction aspect. I think it's better practice for our parking to
be decoupled from housing.*
-Maria Wardoku

Developmental practices and city zoning codes require
developers to build a minimum number of parking spaces when
developing new spaces. These requirements tend to call for one
space per unit, assuming every tenant has a car and need for the
parking spaces. This forces all future renters or buyers to pay for the
parking indirectly regardless of their situations. According to Litman
(2019), developers that factor in one parking space per unit increase
the cost by 12.5%, and two parking spaces per unit increasing the
price by nearly 25%. When looking at low income housing
developments, many of the people who occupy these spaces tend to
own fewer cars.

In addition, these requirements lead to a limited amount of
urban areas that can be used for housing developments (Jaffe, 2019).
For example, in L.A. county, 14 percent of all land is devoted to
parking, the percentage increasing to 40 in downtown Detroit. This
results in an amount of parking that succeeds the needs of the city
(Jaffe, 2019). Referring to the photo below, an overwhelming

amount of urban land is devoted to parking and could be used in a much more efficient way to benefit all people. These spaces should be mixed-use developments, with commercial and residential spaces to allow for the minimization of transportation costs and meet the needs of the people living in these areas (Litman, 2019).

Photo retrieved from Litman (2019).

In Portland, a new model of zoning for mid-density areas is being explored. According to Andersen et al. (2019), if off-street parking is required, developers will build ten townhomes that could sell for nearly $700,000 apiece. If these parking spots are not required, the developers will choose a more profitable route of building a multi-family residential space with twenty-eight condos, each $280,000, with four affordable housing units sold at a price that is below-market value (Andersen et al., 2019). With both space and price in mind, current practices of parking development make housing less accessible, more expensive, and creates an overall inequitable system.

Maria Wardoku also discussed this unjust system and offered other benefits gained from a new arrangement of future development that removes parking from its center. Maria currently works in transportation planning, but previously worked for the University of Minnesota as a graduate researcher with the task of investigating different housing developments within the suburbs of Minneapolis-St. Paul, gathering information about them, diving deeper into developments that were different and offered something to learn from.

Maria helped develop a report called Healthy and Equitable Development: Trends and Possibilities in the Suburbs. This report included suggestions for overcoming obstacles that prevent developments in the suburbs from being healthier and more equitable. The report breaks down these suggestions into three categories; Community Engagement, Active Living, and Equity and Affordable Housing. One development investigated within this report was PLACE. Maria said PLACE was, "…different from everything else…in a class of its own, and very comprehensive in their thinking, linking environment, food, energy, and housing for people with lower incomes, live-work space for creatives, community involvement, and all those things."

Looking closer at the "Active Living" category of the Healthy and Equitable Development report, it is apparent that sidewalks and bike trails can offer an alternative to driving. More focus and attention given to sidewalks and bike paths would lead to less people needing cars, lower the need for parking, and create a more healthy community. Maria discussed that bike lanes must be more than just a small stripe on a busy road, because in order to have a higher percentage of the community utilizing the bike lanes, we must make them more accessible for all ages and abilities. With an increased emphasis on walking and biking, the demand for automobile infrastructure decreases. An interesting effect of this would be an overall shift towards more affordable rent. Maria discussed how housing and transportation tend to be the two biggest expenses for people and how they are extremely intertwined together. If all things within a community were accessible by walking, biking, or public transportation, the overall need for parking would plummet and so would the average price for housing in that area.

Jaffe (2019) offers some solutions rooted in policy change that have the potential to create a more equitable, inclusive environment for housing in our communities. Here are two of these solutions:

1. Eliminate Parking Premiums
    a. Abolish parking requirements for future developments and reform zoning codes
2. Improve Driving Alternatives
    a. Reducing the need of owning a car by building infrastructure that supports bike networks, transit, and walkable neighborhoods.

There may not be one true solution, but housing access can be greatly relieved if more thoughtful approaches are taken when discussing parking. The City of Minneapolis adopted a resolution on October 25th, 2019 to approve a comprehensive strategic plan entitled, Minneapolis 2040. This plan goes into effect January 1st, 2020 and was made to "undo barriers and overcome inequities created by a history of policies in our city that have prevented equitable access to housing, jobs, and investments." By prioritizing walking first, then transit use and bicycling, with motor vehicle last, the city can eliminate racial disparities, more fully address climate change, and deliver a more affordable, equitable housing market.

Maria believes that a big part of tackling these housing issues lies within electing political leaders that can weather the storm, because with any change that happens in the community, there are people who see it as the end of everything. She says political leaders should be making decisions for the greater good of the community rather than listening to those who have the most prominent voice. In addition, communities that are closer and work together will be able to make positive change more easily.

About the author – Logan Monahan

I am a student at the University of St. Thomas studying Neuroscience with a minor in Justice and Peace Studies. I plan on pursuing a career in health care after graduation. I would like to incorporate my interdisciplinary background to lift the voices of the oppressed and create a more just and equitable system of health care in our society.

Works Cited

Andersen, M., Andersen, M., Duncan, T., Andersen, M., Bridges, M. L., Schultz, S., … Andersen, M. (2019, October 30). In Mid-Density Zones, Portland Has a Choice: Garages or Low Prices? Retrieved from https://www.sightline.org/2019/10/02/in-mid-density-zones-portland-has-a-choice-garages-or-low-prices/.

Center for Urban and Regional Affairs. Healthy and Equitable Development: Trends and Possibilites in the Suburbs, (2017, April). Retrieved October 2019, from http://www.cura.umn.edu/news/healthy-and-equitable-development-trends-and-possibilites-suburbs.

Jaffe, E. (2019, October 18). Less parking can mean more housing. Here's how. Retrieved from https://medium.com/sidewalk-talk/less-parking-can-mean-more-housing-heres-how-14b9e50fe646.

Litman, T. (2019). Parking Requirement Impacts on Housing Affordability. Victoria Transport Policy Institute. Retrieved from: https://www.vtpi.org/park-hou.pdf

Welcome to Minneapolis 2040. (2019). Retrieved from https://minneapolis2040.com/.

Art as Community Building

Jamie Marshall has always had a love for the arts. As an undergraduate student at St. Olaf College he participated in the choir and through his love for music knew that he wanted to stay involved in the arts community in some way after graduation. With this goal in mind, Jamie found the organization St. Louis Park Friends of the Arts. He felt immediately drawn to the organization because of its nimble structure that was the antithesis of a large bureaucratic organization and allowed for much flexibility within it. He also found that it made way for him to follow his passion for the arts while also allowing him to follow another passion; building community between one another. Jamie soon found that art was a unique and effective way to do so and is now St. Louis Park Friends of the Art's sole full time staff member as the organization's executive director. In this role, he is able to work within every facet of the organization towards his goal of building community while fostering a greater love for the arts within his area.

The organization St. Louis Park Friends of the Arts began as a community initiative when the school system within St. Louis Park tried to remove the arts programs from the curriculum. In response to this, community members got together to show their support for the arts and their belief in the importance of keeping art alive within their community. As a result, they formed the organization Friends of the Arts around these ideals. In his book Leading Change, Marshall Ganz explains that to make effective change, leaders "learn to form interpersonal relationships that link individuals, networks, and organizations" (Ganz, 2009). The individuals who started this organization sought to form these interpersonal relationships through the creation of art and in doing so were able to link the community and incite change in the role that art played within St. Louis Park. Today, St. Louis Park Friends of the Arts still functions as an avenue to relay the importance of art and to link the greater community through programs such as music initiatives, artist showcases, and poetry readings.

While the organization serves to showcase the arts and its importance within St. Louis Park its main goal in instituting these various arts-based initiatives is to use art as a way to build and foster a sense of community. Jamie explained that "building community through the arts is sort of the motto of the organization" and that at its core it is about "using the arts as a way to bring people together." As a part of his work in his book The Moral Imagination, John Paul Lederach discusses a concept which he refers to as the "pursuit of the creative act." This theory on peacebuilding involves art as a medium for change making by providing an avenue to not only engage with others, but as a way to capture the complexity behind these human experiences. In his book Lederach explains that not only does pursuing the creative act "capture the depth of the challenge" but also "casts light on the way forward" (Lederach, 2005). Lederach believes that by pursuing the creative act within a peace building framework it may supply an individual with a creative lens to work through and provides an unconventional and effective way to make change. In this way Lederach's concept of "pursuing the creative act" supports the objectives of both Jamie and St. Louis Park Friends of the Arts through supplying a theoretical framework that is directly in line with fostering community through an arts-based lens.

One may see Lederach's theory exemplified in the community building work that is done by Friends of the Arts on a daily basis. Through their arts-based projects the organization utilizes this idea of the "pursuit of the creative act" in order to bring people together from all over St. Louis Park. Jamie cited an example of an initiative that the organization put forth that did just this which he referred to as the "community mandala mosaic mural." This project brought in mosaic artists who ran a number of workshops throughout the summer where people from all over the community came and made small circular mosaics. At the end of the summer all of these small works of art were used as pieces to make a larger mosaic mural that was placed in a visible area of St. Louis Park. The community Mandala project that Friends of the Arts conducted works in tandem with this theory in working to capture what Lederach refers to as "the complexity of an organic whole by reaching its simplest composition" (Lederach, 2005). In taking small pieces of art from members all over the community and placing them into a much larger mural, friends of the arts took the complexities of a larger community and brought them together more simply to form one image. In this way, Friends of the Arts utilized the creative act in their work to build a stronger sense of community between the residents of St. Louis Park.

The mandala mosaic mural also served another purpose within the community. Marshall Ganz states that in leadership sometimes we must tell "a story of us", this project served to tell this story which "expresses the values, and the experiences, shared by the us we are evoking at the time" (Ganz, 2009). However, he also states that the story "requires a storyteller, an interpreter of their shared experience" (Ganz, 2009). In this way the Mandela Mosaic Mural sought to tell the community's story of "us" with art being the storyteller. Jamie stated that he believes that this is just one way that Friends of The Arts was able to utilize art to bring people together and foster a strong sense of community, saying that "I think that the arts are a tool for creating community" in that "the arts are often a tool for highlighting sort of the values of a community." In this way the mandala project showcased the collective story of St. Louis Park by sharing the value they place on the arts as a strong facet of their community, and also the importance of coming together to create with one another.

Photo credit: Jamie Marshall

As exemplified in the community mandala project put on by the organization, Lederach's theory of "pursuing the creative act" is at the very foundation of St. Louis Park Friends of the Arts. In his book Lederach explains that "social change that sticks and makes a difference has behind it the artist's intuition: the complexity of human experience captured in a simple image and in a way that moves individuals and whole societies" (Lederach, 2005). Through his work in community building as the Executive Director of St. Louis Park Friends of the Arts, Jamie Marshall and the organization itself are heavily entrenched within the greater St. Louis Park community. It is through these arts-based initiatives that the organization Friends of the Arts works to make a difference by capturing the complexities of their community in simpler forms including that of music, written word, and physical works of art. In this way, Jamie's leadership with this organization has been able to "move" individuals and the greater society, subsequently fostering community in a way that has led to social change within their area. However, Jamie believes that art not only plays an important part in bringing people together but also intersects with many different justice issues that are relevant within St. Louis Park as well. Jamie relayed that he believed that housing justice was an important issue within the artist community in that it is oftentimes hard for artists to find housing that they are able to afford "so designing spaces that are intended for artists to be in and stay in is really important." He also believes that it this is an important issue for the greater community as a whole saying that "housing options for everyone who wants to be a part of the community, I should say, is a priority for the city right now."

Jamie believes that the work that PLACE is hoping to do within St. Louis Park will aid in addressing this justice issue of affordable housing within the community. However, while PLACE may act to serve residents of the community, he believes that Friends of the Arts can also work to act as a bridge between PLACE and St. Louis Park. Jamie stated that through the leadership of Friends of the Arts and PLACE coming together there will be a kind of cyclical relationship between the two organizations. He believes that PLACE will greatly impact the artist community in St. Louis Park and therefore grow the arts within the community through giving a space to "a bunch more artists, but a bunch of artists in a place that connects them." In turn he believes this will strengthen the arts within the area in that "It could give a sort of central location, physical location for the arts in St. Louis Park, which right now doesn't really exist, we don't have an art center… so I think this sort of becomes that natural central location." In this way PLACE may offer a new artists hub for the area, benefiting the community. In terms of his organization he stated that because "the St. Louis Park arts community is already here and strong" Friends of the Arts may use their engagement within the community, along with art as a medium to foster greater connection within PLACE and its relationship to the St. Louis Park residents.

Lederach's concept of "pursuing the creative act" serves not only as a theoretical framework that supports St. Louis Park Friends of the Arts, but is applicable to the work that PLACE is doing in conjunction with the organization as well. By supplying a kind of central location for artists to connect within their building, PLACE is aiding in the growth of the St. Louis Park arts community as a whole. This specific focus is very much in line with Lederach's theory as he states in his work that "in the process of professionalization we too often have lost a sense of the art, the creative act that underpins the birth and growth of personal and social change" (Lederach, 2005). Both PLACE and Friends of the Arts are organizations that while professional in nature, have seen the importance of a sense of art and creativity despite the process of professionalization. Both organizations value the creative act and in doing so are working together to foster a growth of the arts community in St. Louis Park, while bringing residents together as a result. Although utilizing different avenues, St. Louis Park Friends of the Arts and PLACE intersect with Lederach's theory of the "pursuit of the creative act" and through this shared value of creativity they are agents of change within their community.

About the Author - Emilie Dozer

I am a Justice and Peace Studies and Sociology major at the University of St. Thomas. I have a passion for learning about the arts community and the work that individuals are doing here in the Twin Cities to combine arts and community building. That being said, I loved being able to explore this further within the context of this chapter!

Works Cited

Ganz, Marshall. 2009. "Leading Change" Handbook of Leadership Theory and Practice: A Harvard Business School Centennial Colloquium. Boston, MA: Harvard Business Press.

Lederach, John Paul. 2005. "On Aesthetics" The Moral Imagination. New York, NY: Oxford University Press.

Marshall, Jamie. (2019 October 31.) personal interview.

What Role Does Art Play in A Community?

Art and finding our way back to our humanity are connected...To believe in healing is to believe in the creative act
- John Paul Lederach

Symone Wilson identifies as a woman of color, a part of the LGBTQA+ community, a loving daughter of two actors, and an activist for the art community. Her story started out by mentioning her hardworking family and how this has transpired into her own work ethic. Her many jobs revolve around nonprofits and helping other artists on the business side of building a portfolio. What connects Ms. Wilson to PLACE is United Artist Collaboration, she is the reason these two non-profits are now working together. Her job here is to help local Minnesota artists promote and market their artwork. This includes funding for marketing, supplies, hosting shows at different venues, etc. She stated, "I focus heavily on trying to raise others that can relate to me that feel like they're outsiders that feel like they don't have a place to belong". She sees a living space as security, magic, and the sense of belonging that comes from a home. Though, while working multiple jobs she is still unable to afford her own car and a place to call her own.

When mentioning her first childhood memory of her home, she used the word "magic." She stated, "the first house that I lived in was really special to me and anytime I think back on it, it's like a place of magic in my heart." She later remembers when this "magic" was taken away from her and her family when they had to file for bankruptcy. She stated, "I was very sad, I felt like I was ashamed when we moved into an apartment. I was ashamed that my parents had to go through bankruptcy. My parents were like 'don't tell anybody', because I believe that they were ashamed too." Being ashamed of where you live is deeper than a physical appearance. A house is more than a roof over your head, it is a place of belonging in a community. The emotional feeling of loss is something that Ms. Wilson will always carry. Evan if her family is financial stable, the uncertainty of what could happen will be a lingering fear constantly in your mind. She mentioned that her parent asked her to keep the move a secret. She states, "But I think that keeping it a secret causes more problems and bringing it to light can make people realize that we should not have to go through this as artists as people of color and as women." In a supportive community you should not have to lie about where you live. As a society we should not judge others on their financial stability and deem them unworthy because they are not your same profession. The importance of owning a home goes beyond having a place to express yourself, feel safe, and keep warm. Owning a home builds financial stability for future generations so they too can own their own home and create equity for themselves and their children. The equity gained from a home is money that can be passed on to your children after you have passed. This then creates financial stability so they can give their children a better education and build an even stronger community in the future.

This story is not about the hardships of having to move after going bankrupt as a family, it is about the reason as to why this happened how it happened, and what outside sources has our society created for this to happen. There is segregation in our housing system, especially here in Minnesota and in Saint Louis Park. When it comes to injustice in our housing system it is almost impossible to not look at racism and what role this plays historically and in today's social justice issues. It is not a coincidence that white people live in more suburban areas and people of color live in smaller homes or apartments closer to highways or in more "dangerous" parts of town. In previous chapters, the redlining and housing covenants shows the effects racism has had on building our communities. As a society, we continue to feed into this system and this is part of issues that Symone saw PLACE trying to address when she became an advocate for them and linked them to the non-profits she works for, United Artist Collaboration. If both parents with college educations have jobs in a family of four, but their wages do not add up enough for them to have a home for their family, this is a real issue in our community that needs to be addressed.

One of the most beautiful things Symone said was what she would picture as the perfect situation for her community. She did not specify anything of monetary value or a bundle of free houses, she pictures an artistic community that thrived off one another. She stated, "I want to buy a city, and we all (artists) just move down there to create our own artistic community. It would be very vibrant, not even colorful, that it would be a mass filled with singers, dancers, artist all living together. We could have the prettiest neighborhoods, with color everywhere. It would be beautiful." What would this look like as a community? Who would this benefit? It would not only benefit the artist that live there, but a life filled with art including music, dance, painting, drawing, singing, and simply expression help a child find their own identity. It helps a child, adult and anyone in between look at what inspires them and what they are passionate about. When you are passionate about something you do your best work, you do the most research, and you work hard. There is no other outcome. A community fully committed to what they do and helping others is what we see education as. It is what we see thriving businesses as. Yet, we see housing as a simple way of life and ignore the injustice in our housing system simply because it does not affect us, we are unknowledgeable about it, or we see our housing system as something unchangeable, when it is. This is what PLACE is trying to do.

Ms. Wilson's story may seem simple, a family losing a house, filing for bankruptcy, and then gaining the funds to buy another house. This may even look like a success story. The underlying reasons as to why she and many other artists, people of color, people who identify with the LGBTQA+ community, people who are non-binary, or people who prefer to label owning a home as a "white mans" dream is because we have continued to play into this cycle. If you feel shame as a parent for losing a home or not being financially stable it affects you emotional, mentally, and physically. People also tend to see artists as free entertainment and nothing but a dream when the artist themselves know that their passion is their livelihood. As a working local artist or an artist starting to build a portfolio, the pay is very low, so low that having one job or even two is not enough to cover your bills. Why should people have to choose between doing what you love and being below middle class? Why can we not have happiness, passion, and love in our work? Why do we not create communities filled with affordable homes that allow multiple income classes to purchase them?

These questions do not seem hard to answer, yet we do not have solutions and we do not ask these questions. A home is meant to build a family, create a safe place for an individual or many to rest, stay warm, and express their culture. A community builds relationships, trust, grassroots, families, and a safe place for you to just be. Why does a home in this community seem so unattainable for someone with a college degree and three jobs? Or a family of four with two hardworking adults? These are questions PLACE is trying to answer, in a way that changes how we see, art, community, and housing. How can PLACE use art and community to build healing and reflection for not only its residents, but the surrounding communities?

Symone Wilson sees art as a way to express herself and her love for music. She also sees art as a way to build a strong community. Art can be used to preserve history and create healing.

Art is a form of expression and it can sometimes be the loudest voice in the room, yet makes no noise. A song can be the quietest melody and still create emotion, and a dance can a tell a story, yet no one is talking. That is the power of art. The idea of seeing art as a way to build a community is similar to how John Paul Lederach illuminates the connection between art, community, growth, and healing.

John Paul Lederach became the founding director for the Center for Justice and Peacebuilding at Eastern Mennonite University where he was a professor. A lot of his work has focused on the importance of grassroots organizing and how this builds a community. Lederach embraces the idea that art can change a community and that music can help lead escalating conflicts into resolutions and even stop violent wars from happening. In his book, The Moral Imagination: The Art and Soul of Building Peace, Lederach mentions artful change and how the simple sound of music can make someone stop and think, but also be used as a peaceful tactic to create disruption. When he was at conference in Ireland in 1996, he mentioned that he could not remember a single speech, proposal, or formal panel response, but he could remember the five-minute performance of Paul Brandy's "The Island", the photos that were projected behind him, and the women dancing. He stated, "I do however, remember, vividly, the image and feeling of those five minutes of combined music, lyrics, choreography, and photos. It created an echo in my head that has not gone away. It moved me" (Lederach). When you hear music or encounter any type of art form everyone's reaction is different. It creates an emotional connection and memory for you to hold on to. This is important to understand when talking about a community and a home, memories do not just carry images of the past, they carry emotions and feelings that stay with you forever.

When talking about the social injustices in our housing system, people recognize the financial struggle of owning a home, but the political and social barriers are what need to be focused on.

Music is a way to find peace and create an emotional connection with the people around you. Lederach states, "music, it seems, has the power to push things either in the direction of greater violence or towards reconciliation" (Lederach). and that "elegance and beauty are often captured when complexity is reflected in the simplest of lines, curves, textures, melodies, or rhythms. Reconciliation that is framed as an intellectually complex process will too often create so much noise and distraction that the essence is missed" (Lederach). Music is not solely for expression, art itself is a way to heal and build communities. When art is presented it brings different types of emotions to every single person that experiences it. Music can entrance you to listen to the melody or to the beat, it can slow down your heart or make it speed up. The lyrics, if they are presented, can stop and make you think, you can resonate with what the artists are trying to say because art has one of the most powerful voices.

Lederach states that "we must find a way to touch the sense of art that lies within us all…Art is a form of love. It is finding beauty and connection in what we do" (Lederach). Love is what fills a home no matter how small. Though, we do not give people a change to have these homes or create these experiences. We have built a system that stops people from embracing art as a lifestyle, and not hobby. We have stopped seeing communities as ways to build trust, relationships, and make change. Any place you call home is where you should feel safe, so we need to make sure everyone has the opportunity to do so. Symone Wilson's passion for art and community is not one sided. Many people want to change how we see music and stop the system that prevents others who are not of a certain class or race from having a safe place to live. We should not have to dream of a community filled with art, creativity, love, diversity, and opportunity should already be a reality.

As mentioned in previous chapters, the idea of PLACE itself seems like a dream; a living space full of different socioeconomic classes living an eco-friendly powered home. Symone Wilson is not only a candidate for living in PLACE she is also the connection PLACE has with creating art filled community with United Artist Collaboration. Her passion for helping others share their music and their voice is something every community needs. PLACE is grasping some of Ms. Wilson's vision of community life. It may not be an entire city, but it is a dream turning into reality.

About the Author - Emma Rose Hendrickson

I am a Business Law and Justice and Peace Studies graduate from the University of Saint Thomas. I am very passionate about art and everything that surrounds it. I have been dancing since the age of two and I love to paint and draw, it helps me communicate with the world and express who I am. I see art as one of the biggest voices in a social movement because of its impact on every individual. I hope to continue to research and continue a career in social justice.

Works Cited

Lederach, J. P. (2010). The Moral Imagination: The Art and Soul of
    Building Peace. New York, NY: Oxford University Press
    Inc. pp. 152-169

Symone Wilson (PLACE Candidate & singer) in discussion with
    author, October 30th, 2019

Home as Heaven

As soon as Jim McDonough locks eyes with me, I know its him. Approaching our meeting I have only learned of his vibrant and extensive experience in local advocacy from his online LinkedIn profile, but his aura signals a parallel energy. McDonough is a seemingly quirky, artistic gentleman fitted in a tastefully multi-patterned suit at first glance; and an hour later our conversation reveals a plethora of intriguing experiences from the frontlines of grassroots housing and economic justice organizations in Minneapolis, spanning decades.

The conversation meanders from his undergraduate experience at the University of St. Thomas, to his various jobs within the Twin Cities, to his personal experiences with housing and pretty soon it is clear: we could talk for days. Not only does he have a breadth of experience in local advocacy bridging decades, but his gentle fervor makes for contagious intrigue. I found myself wanting so much more time than we had to excavate the deeply personal motivations for his advocacy.

McDonough, a board member of Park Theater Company in St. Louis Park, serves as a liaison to a neighborhood group called Friends of the Arts that landed him a seat at a July 2016 informational meeting for the PLACE (Projects Linking Arts Community and Environment) project. He shares with me how it felt to hear about the multi-unit housing development with plans for an outdoor amphitheater, an indoor theater, and workspace for artists.

At this point in our conversation, McDonough's countenance lit up, "I thought I had died and gone to heaven...it sounded exactly like the kind of community not only that I'd want to support but that I'd want to live in."

McDonough continues to describe how he feels about PLACE in glowing terms, and what catches my attention is how distinct his descriptions of PLACE are from any other housing he recounts having in his life. McDonough bought his first house 45 years ago and still lives in that first purchase to this day. He talks about downsizing and the consideration many have at one point in their life to strive for a more perfect fit. The difference I see between PLACE and other housing opportunities he has described having evokes the idea of a house as one's true home, and further being one's heaven. Though he is grateful, McDonough describes his current home as a burden, due to the exponentially growing property tax and a heavy mortgage with a substantial interest rate, "It's a little too much for me at my stage in life as a single-person-homeowner to shoulder." As our conversation continues, he uses more language that emphasizes the heavy burden homeownership is, and how he is searching for relief from this weight.

McDonough shares more about his past, and here I learn a life lesson: the difference between a house and a home. For Jim, being involved in one's community was never an option: "It just seemed it was part of our family deal to be part of whatever particular activities were involved with the church." Watching his parents' dedication to their religious community and neighborhood influenced Jim's affinity for leadership, and eventually political activism.

His participation in the long struggle for social change began in the 60s and 70s as a student. Serving in the seminary for five and a half years, he encountered a time of great social upheaval within the Catholic Church. He eventually discerned out of the seminary, not feeling called to the priesthood, and transferred to the University of St. Thomas, where he studied Psychology and graduated in 1969. "As a seminarian in the early and mid 60s, it was a great time of social change and structural change within the church itself." Starting with the Civil Rights and anti-war movements, Jim describes involvement after involvement throughout his life as an undergraduate and graduate student, increasing his leadership in the community.

This is where I begin to see him describing a real application of the aforementioned Circle of Praxis. The movements he got involved with as a student were a catalyst for his desire to improve his community, or as an exposure to injustice. After undergraduate, his exposure to the issues of housing insecurity and affordability and economic injustice became more personal. McDonough went on to complete a doctoral degree in 1975 in Clinical Psychology with minors in Child Development and Statistics at the University of Minnesota, where he engaged in more descriptive analysis of the systems surrounding him.

McDonough highlighted many of the problems PLACE is addressing as prominent concerns in his own life: environmental stewardship, economic justice, and housing as an aspect of social justice. Within Minneapolis alone, McDonough has been "actively involved with the issues of gainful employment and affordable housing as a human services provider", serving on the Human Services Committee, 15 years on the Human Rights Commission, as president of the Minnesota League of Human Rights, and several other organizations and initiatives seeking justice over the course of his career. Namely, McDonough articulates progressive work done during his time on the West Hennepin Human Services Board, advising the county commissioners on issues of affordable housing and homelessness.

I begin to plot the plethora of experiences McDonough carries humbly in my mental diagram of the social change wheel, realizing just how meaningful and encompassing his work has been.

He recounts a position he held working with a shelter organization called Alliance of the Streets as particularly moving. Solidifying a calling to serve members of his community experiencing homelessness, his job was specifically to find work for the people staying in the shelter. McDonough confronts the misconceptions we often hear about the undeserving poor. "'Jeez, how do those people get in that situation? You know, they're just lazy. Why don't they go out and get another job?' Most of the people on the streets that are homeless do work I would guarantee that, that was my job to find them [a job]." McDonough continues to engage in social analysis, engaging his academic knowledge and professional experience to challenge these stereotypes.

As Jim goes on, he continues a normative analysis of the US economic system. Highly critical of economic inequality in our society, McDonough argues that even if someone has a steady job, housing still may be inaccessible, "Why is affordable housing so critical? Because the wages have not grown commensurate with the cost of living." McDonough confidently asserts the inequities that are rampant in our economic system, "I always cringed a little and still do when people talk about well, you got to pull yourself up by your bootstraps... All of us are only one or two paychecks away from a crisis." McDonough does not miss a beat to emphasize that "these issues that we're talking about employment, unemployment, housing, homelessness, there is also are very much a racial component to them" highlighting those on the social margins in an already marginalized economic group.

This near-crisis normal that we have accepted is what prevents many of us from seeking a home among our house. If we work overtime and can barely afford rent, there will not be time or energy to build a community or lead like McDonough has been able to. The kind of exploitative capitalism that keeps many working-class Americans too afraid to lose their job to assert their needs or values is exactly the kind of economic system that prevents people from building and sustaining community to keep them healthy and happy. McDonough highlights negative trends throughout history by recounting minute details of how much his first wages were, how much his first car cost, how much his first apartment cost, and how vastly different and nearly impossible these expenses are today for most people. Statistics and dates coming easily to him, his message is clear: our economic system is failing us.

In addition to recounting the challenges and failures, what I also hear from McDonough is a chronicle of resistance, a narrative of collective liberation, and a case for action (the final step in the circle of praxis). Between all his positions within Minneapolis, McDonough has demonstrated how one person can dedicate time to several aspects of the social change wheel; he alone has participated in grassroots organizing, public policy work, community building, and economic development several times over (as well as other spokes on the wheel we simply did not have time to cover in our conversation). Inspired by his parents' active roles in their community and the social upheaval of the 60s, his narrative swells around the importance of action: "There's a difference between saying the words and doing the work. Yes, good. intentions are good, but it takes it takes more it takes understanding. It takes a dedication, and a commitment." Through his humility I can see his impact stretching across Minneapolis, as small yet powerful acts of solidarity and support for his community: of seeking a home within his house and manifesting a collective home within his city.

As someone who has spent countless hours and immeasurable energy working toward a more just economic system, it makes perfect sense how desirable PLACE is to McDonough. Informed by experiences of injustice and motivated by grassroots work toward economic equality, McDonough has conceptualized an idea of home as heaven, and spent years working toward this goal for members of his community. PLACE is his chance to actualize a heavenly home for himself.

Certainly, I heard many well-informed critiques of the US economic system and feel provoked by his assessment of the failures in wages and housing, but I also heard a call to the individual. This call beckons to each person with a passion for social change, asking how we will commit ourselves to complete service of our community. How will we make our cities into our homes, and our homes into heaven, providing for the needs of all our cohabitants?

About the Author – Elizabeth Stephenson

I will graduate from the University of St. Thomas, MN in May of 2020 with a BA in English and Justice & Peace Studies and a minor in American Culture and Difference. Pursuing a vocational calling into the field of education, I plan to attend graduate school to study higher education and student affairs. Ultimately, I seek to actualize social justice by challenging internalized superiority, eliminating apathy, and igniting communities for collective liberation. I am deeply passionate about writing poetry, riding trains, and falling off my longboard.

Works Cited

McDonough, Jim. (2019, October 28.) personal interview.

Epilogue

In December 2019, the second phase of Via (Via Luna) came to an end. There seems much that could be said on the subject of how and why it ended, but PLACE is intent on directing its energy to the here and now, which entails the construction of the first phase of Via (Via Sol). PLACE acknowledges that—with all the years of engagement, planning, design, and other hard work put into Via Luna by so many in the community—it was hard to lose this opportunity. Yet, PLACE understands that, in the fight to create vibrant, healthy, and sustainable living opportunities for folks all along the income spectrum, pressing on is paramount. Included below is a letter from PLACE to key supporters in the community following the end of Via Luna.

"Thank you for supporting our transit-oriented community in St. Louis Park known as Via. We have good news and sad news to share, and, as one of our key supporters for Via, we wanted to reach out to you before the broader announcements are made.

The good news is that construction is moving full speed on the north residential building (Via Sol). Opening in July 2021, it will bring 217 new affordable and market-rate apartments, 18 of which will be live/work for creatives. The building is interwoven with several spaces around the inside and outside for residents to share their work, and the Urban Art Forest will feature rotating installations from local and national artists.

PLACE's renewable food and energy program (E-Generation) will still bring solar PV panels, a wind turbine, a solar PV + green hybrid roof, anaerobic digestion for organic waste, a greenhouse offering organic produce year-round, and workshops by Spark-Y focused on healthy, sustainable living. This too will open next summer and power Via Sol.

Our project, even by the standard of affordable developments, has been hit by an unusual number of challenges, from the site changing multiple times, to having our funding interrupted by the Tax Cuts and Jobs Act of 2017. Most recently, the $50 million second phase of the Via community was forced to halt just ten weeks from breaking ground when we were unable to meet new requirements imposed by the City.

PLACE, a 501(c)(3) nonprofit dedicated to the creation of mixed-use, mixed-income, transit-oriented communities, planned a campus surrounding the new Wooddale Station, with the second phase bringing fifty live and work suites for creatives and their families, affordable to households earning 60% of the area's median income. We had already received funding through the State of Minnesota's MMB tax-exempt bond program for affordable housing. Also included was a community theater, creative co-working space, a cafe, a coffeehouse, a neighborhood rooftop bar, the Arts & Transit Plaza, and a Marriott 110-room arts hotel that hired community members for living-wage jobs. The project was seeking a Gold environmental design award through the LEED program.

The second phase of our project had also received an $850,000 Transit Oriented Development grant from the Met Council to support an art and transit plaza for placemaking. Along with the Met Council, Hennepin County, LISC, and Minnesota's DEED office had supported the project, which would have reclaimed a blighted brownfield, with support for environmental cleanup.

The loss of the second phase has been difficult for everyone at PLACE and for our project team as we all worked very hard to make it a reality. We still feel that an art-focused, job-creating, environmentally sustainable vision accessible to people across the income spectrum and filled with community space is a good fit for this location, and we hope whatever is chosen for this site brings meaningful benefits to the entire community.

We appreciate your continued support as we move forward with Via Sol and E-Generation, working even harder to build something that will help our residents and the surrounding community thrive."

The student authors wish the very best to PLACE and to the City of St. Louis Park as they strive to promote leadership for social justice in housing in the best interests of current and future residents.

Course Assignment Instructions

The stories collected in this volume were premised on the pedagogical foundations above and structured by the assignment instructions and rubrics below. Students completed their stories in three steps (A-C):

☐ Part A. Identify and Engage - Story Inventory Assignment
☐ Part B. Describe Voice of People and Purpose through Story
☐ Part C. Analyze Leadership for Social Justice by Applying Theory

The assignments are included here to provide context for the structure behind student leadership stories, and in the hope that they might inspire applications for other courses.

Part A. Identify and Engage - Story Inventory Assignment

Instructions: Complete each section below by typing directly into this document. You can add lines as you type, expanding the length as necessary. Use the first draft to take make detailed notes, and the second draft to edit for clarity and coherence. **Bring a rough draft to class on [date].** Submit a **final draft** via email in this format: **LASTNAME.doc by [date - one week later].**

> Objectives:
> - ☐ Exploring key questions about your story
> - ☐ Confirming the social justice orientation of your story
> - ☐ Focusing the story you will tell in your story - distilling a complex experience into a meaningful narrative
> - ☐ Identifying a realistic and reasonable subject for your story and anticipating issues of access and ethics

1. Leadership Focus:

Who or what are you profiling?

Given the freedom to choose any leadership story, why did you choose this one?

What do you find meaningful in this example that you hope might inspire others?

2. Leadership Story:

What is the story of this person/group/campaign/organization/movement?

How does their **Story of Self** (individually or collectively) connect to a larger **Story of Us**?

Describe the identity of the person/group/campaign/organization/movement in leadership.

How does their **Voice** help you understand social justice in a different way?

3. Leadership Dynamics:

How does power operate in the leadership you are profiling?

Who is involved in **Decision-making?**

How is leadership organized (i.e.: vertical or horizontal structure)?

4. Leadership in Action:

What is the social justice goal?

What **strategies** are used to achieve the goal?

What **tactics** emerge from the strategies?

How does the mission align with daily action?

How does leadership work with other in **collective action**?

<u>5. Leadership Context(s)</u>
How does identity and social location(s) impact their work for social justice?
Is leadership occurring in the context of a local/community project, regional
initiative, national campaign, or international social movement?
How are local and global work coordinated?

<u>6. Experiential Resources for Storytelling - what access do you have to direct and
indirect experiences</u>
What direct resources will you use, i.e.: conversations, participatory events, art
exhibits, protests, public meetings, etc.?
What indirect/mediated resources will you use, i.e.: mass media (i.e.: print, online
content); proprietary documentation (i.e.: brochures, annual reports, press
releases); third-party documentation (i.e.: documentary video, awards and
recognition, academic reports, etc.)?

<u>7. Consent Form</u>
Submit consent form after reading to your subject and receiving signature and date

<u>Rubric for grading</u>
- Great work answers most of the questions in all seven categories with
  detail, clarity, and coherence
- Good work addresses 2 questions in all seven categories with detail,
  clarity, and coherence
- Fair work addresses1-2 questions in all seven categories with limited
  detail, clarity, and coherence
- Poor work addresses only 1 question in all seven categories without
  detail, clarity, or coherence

Part B. Story

Instructions: Complete each section below by typing directly into this document. You can add lines as you type, expanding the length as necessary. Use the first draft to take make detailed notes, and the second draft to edit for clarity and coherence. **Bring a rough draft to class on [date] for peer review**. Submit a **final draft** in this format: **LASTNAMEpartB.doc by [date - one week later]**.

Objectives:
- [ ] Distill data from Part A. into a story that gives voice to the subject of your leadership story
- [ ] Construct the story in three parts: around a conflict, a decision, and an outcome
- [ ] Give voice to your subject's Story of Self, Story of Us, and Story of Now
- [ ] Identify ethical considerations about giving voice to your subject

1. What are the key data from Part A. that help tell the story of your profile? Note the 7-10 most interesting and compelling data here. Imagine your data as beads of different colors, sizes, and shapes that will you string together into a coherent narrative.

2. Construct the Story - arrange on the narrative string of conflict, decision, outcome:
What is the conflict (injustice, violence, oppression or problem)?
What assets (skills, abilities, resources, ideas) does the subject of your profile bring to the conflict?
What decisions did this require of leadership?
What were the outcomes of those decisions?

3. Give voice to your subject (review Ganz, "Why Stories Matter: The Art and Craft of Social Change" and Lederach, "The Moral Imagination")
What is your subject's **Story of Self**? (See Ganz, and Lederach Ch. 2 for guidance)
How does your subject's **Story of Us** connect to larger issues or movements? (See Ganz, and Lederach Ch. 8 - On Space: Life in the Web)
What is it about your subject's **Story of Now** that is compelling for this moment in time? (See Ganz, and Lederach Ch. 3 - On This Moment: Turning Points)

4. Identify ethical considerations about giving voice to your subject
How might your story positively impact your subject?
How might your story negatively impact your subject?

How might your limited experience or limited research of your subject lead to inadequacies in your story? How will you address this limitation?
How might your own normative values color your story, positively or negatively?

5. Accountability
If your subject were to read your story, how would they react to it? How might their imagined reaction change the way you give voice to their story?
At the end of the semester, we will publish these profiles in a book that is publicly accessible. How does this public accessibility impact the way you give voice to their story?

Rubric for grading
- Great work responds to most of the prompts in all five categories with detail, clarity, and coherence
- Good work addresses 2 prompts in all five categories with some detail, clarity, and coherence
- Fair work addresses 1-2 prompts in all five categories with limited detail, clarity, and coherence
- Poor work addresses only 1 prompt in each category without detail, clarity, or coherence

Part C. Theory

Instructions: Complete each section below by typing directly into this document. You can add lines as you type, expanding the length as necessary. Use the first draft to take make detailed notes, and the second draft to edit for clarity and coherence. **Bring a rough draft to class on [date] for peer review**. Submit a **final draft** in this format: **LASTNAMEpartC.doc by [date - one week later]**.

Objectives:

☐ To deepen your understanding of leadership for social justice by applying a course concept to your story

☐ To analyze your story in the light of theory to better understand the dynamics of power

☐ To add theoretical depth to your story to enhance readers' engagement

1. Identify course concepts that might be applied to your story (circle 3-5):

Stages of Team Development	Story of Self/Us/Now (Ganz)
Three Faces of power (Boulding)	Improvisation/Serendipity (Lederach)
Relationship of Identity/Agency	Hegemony/ideology (Gramsci)
Web of Relationships (Lederach)	Paradoxical curiosity (Lederach)
Pursuit of the creative act (Lederach)	Risking nonviolence
(Lederach)	
Asset-based approach (Kretzman)	Ethics of engagement (Illich/Remen)
Critical pedagogy (Freire)	Community organizing
Danger of a Single Story (Adichie)	Creative Tensions in SMOs
Democratizing Leadership (Klein)	Ethics and empathy
(voice/decision-making/collective action)	(values/duties/rights/outcomes)

2. Research your chosen concepts from our readings and your class notes.
Choose one concept that helps to explain your story:
Story of Self/Us,
Describe this concept:
How does this concept help explain your profile?

3. Identify the key data from Part A. or B. that connect this concept to your story?
Note the 4-6 most interesting and compelling data that connect to course concepts:

4. Using numbers 1-3 above, write a concise essay (2-4 pages) using your chosen concept to explain leadership for social justice in your story.

- ☐ Describe your concept (with appropriate citations and references in APA format) - you may use sources from class and from research outside of class
- ☐ Use your concept to explain leadership for social justice in your story
- ☐ Give examples of this concept in action through data you've collected (quotes, statistics, mission statements, organizational structure, decision-making processes, etc.) and/or your story (quotes, anecdotes, situations, questions, etc.)
- ☐ Conclude with a summary states the significance of your concept for explaining leadership for social justice in this story and how it might apply to other examples (implications/applications)

Rubric for grading

- Great work describes the concept clearly with citations, explains leadership for social justice in the profile coherently, provides detailed examples, and concludes with multiple applications beyond this profile
- Good work describes the concept with citations, explains leadership for social justice in the profile, provides examples, and concludes with a single application beyond this profile
- Fair work describes the concept, explains leadership for social justice in the profile, provides an example, and concludes with a single application beyond this profile
- Poor work describes the concept without clarity, describes but does not explain leadership for social justice in the profile, provides a vague example, and concludes without clear application beyond this profile

Index

About the Editor

Mike Klein, Ed.D. is an Associate Professor and Program Director of Justice and Peace Studies at the University of St. Thomas. He teaches undergraduate courses in Leadership for Social Justice, Qualitative Research, Introduction to Justice and Peace Studies; and seminars in art and social change, historical interpretation for contemporary justice, and coffee as lens for interdisciplinary analysis. He also teaches graduate courses on social justice pedagogy, critical education in social movements, and the pedagogy of Paulo Freire. His research, publishing, and consulting focus on: democratizing leadership, peace education, popular culture, intersections of art and social justice, and peacebuilding. He develops the agency of students and communities for transforming structures to advance social justice.

Other Books by Mike Klein:

Leadership for Social Justice, Volumes I - VI (Editor)
Democratizing Leadership: Counter-Hegemonic Democracy in Organizations, Institutions, and Communities (Author)
Neighborhood Leadership: Celebrating Twenty-five Years of the Neighborhood Leadership Program (with Damon Shoholm)
Teaching a Peace of my Mind: Exploring the Meaning of Peace One Story at a Time (Author)
Teaching the Compassionate Rebel Revolution: Ordinary People Changing the World (Editor)